Cathy, brought up in a 'comf[...] at the age of seven, suddenly [...] as a baby and assured by her m[...] had given birth to her loved her but had made the difficult decision that she would be better off being brought up by others. Having been told this at the age of seven Cathy seemed to take it in her stride, as children do, though questions began to rise and recur about her own mother, she kept them to herself.

Then, in her early teens, she developed a heart condition and doctors felt information on her genetic background would be of help. Once more health problems came to light as an adult, and Cathy, in an age before such research became so fashionable, and thanks to the internet, so much easier, started on a quest to discover her true roots. The resulting journey, bringing us almost to the present day, resulted in the discovery of a large and vibrant extended family on her birth-father's side, touched upon The Nuremburg Trials. Her father's travels and work in South America, Africa and South Africa, took her on a journey of discovery to his last home in South Africa and culminated in the bitter-sweet discovery, after years of dead ends, that she might well have passed her late mother unrecognised in the streets of the city where she lived, and where Cathy studied at the university.

Cathy felt that she had to write her story, for herself and her children and to support others who may be teetering on the edge of beginning their own journey of discovery. Also, for foster parents, adoptive parents, professionals, and students who might work with or support children and young people in foster care and who may be hoping for their forever home through adoption.

It is clear that for some people like Cathy, they just need to know where they come from, for others perhaps not. Cathy hopes that her story might help other people to take the next step in their own discoveries. There is always a risk of rejection. There can be a tremendous sense of loss and grief when uncovering the past and there needs to be support and help available to cope with those possibilities. There are also many surprises, great happiness, and a very real sense of belonging.

I would like to say a big thank you to all of my family for their support and encouragement in completing this journey. Also, thanks to Andy Bogen for pulling everything together ready to publish.

Out of the Quill Box

Came Secrets of a family
I had never known

Cathy Mayes

Independently Published by Cathy Mayes

First Published 2021 Cathy Mayes

Copyright © 2021, Cathy Mayes

Contact:
cathyfreelance15@outlook.com
Facebook: Cathy Mayes Author
The right of Cathy Mayes to be identified as the author of
this work has been asserted by the publisher in accordance
with the Copyright, Designs and Patents Act 1988.

Chapter Contents

Who am I?

I have two names

My name at birth

My legal name

There was a mother and a father

and then came me, Catherine.

Who am I?

Chapter 1

Opening the Quill Box

I remember so clearly that day ….

When I was about seven years old my mum took me into the sitting room, the door opened inwards and to the left, behind the door was a bookcase. On top of the bookcase there was a box, it was not large, it was inlaid with porcupine quills, and had black lacquered wood inlaid with mother-of-pearl.

I remember standing beside my mum in that space behind that door. I remember what I was wearing, ski-type stretch leggings with the stirrup under the foot, they were dark green with brown and blue stripes, I had a green jumper on, one that my god-mother had knitted for me, she made me one every birthday until I was sixteen. I am not sure where my sisters, Jo and Clare were, perhaps I was at home from school, perhaps they were out. They were not in that room with me and mum. And nor was dad, where was he?

Mum looked at me and said, she had something to tell me, and to show me. She carefully lifted the lid of the box and took some folded papers out. These papers are yours and I need to tell you about them, what they mean, she said. The papers had been given to mum and dad following a court case, when I became their daughter. Mum explained to me that I had another mother before, she was a good person, she was a nurse, twenty-eight years old when she had me, not married. She had wanted to look after me and to keep me, although it became impossible for her, as she was working as a private nurse at the time. My mother had made the difficult decision to let someone else become my mum and for me to have both a mum, and a dad. She thought that would be best for me. My mother's name was Margaret.

My mum and dad had wanted to have another child and decided that adoption (what did that mean?) would be a good idea. I was the child that they chose, and that they would adopt. This is how and why I came to live with them and became their child. Mum suggested that she look after the papers for me and she carefully folded them before she put them back in the box. That as I remember it, was the sum-total of the conversation. I do not remember asking questions and I do not remember mum asking if I had any questions, did she? It was a long time ago.

That was it. As a child I accepted what I was told. I do not remember dad ever mentioning the adoption or asking me about what mum had told me, though I must have assumed that he knew about the conversation. The only time I think that dad referred to the adoption was on my wedding day. I said thank you, for everything, and he said, 'no, I should be thanking you'.

Life went on. I do not remember feeling shocked or surprised, mum had explained that she had been told by the adoption people, that she should tell me as soon as I could understand, so that no-one else told me first. It must have been hard, and perhaps risky for mum to tell me this. I would have needed time to process this information. I cannot understand why I do not remember how I felt, I remember so much other detail, like what I was wearing, the room, the box, standing there, behind the door, I remember those details like it was yesterday, physical rather than emotional. This information must have had a huge impact on me, knowing that I had been chosen and knowing now, that I was different. Different from other children, my friends, and my sisters. I wonder how my sister Jo felt about having a new sister and what impact my arrival may have had for her. Clare came along three years after me and so I imagine it did not have an impact on her. We were sisters all three of us and we still are.

I remember some incidents that happened after this momentous event and I wonder now if there was a link. I was at school with my older sister at that time and I was in big trouble for putting yellow powder paint all over the lovely new green gingham curtains that fronted the cupboards for the art equipment. I was in trouble for this at school, and in trouble when I got home. Apart from my tap-dancing lessons, the outdoor play area, where I once found an injured thrush, and the uniform, I do not remember very much about that school.

I was moved to another school, a little closer to home, within walking distance. I remember the green uniform, the outdoor swimming pool where I was stung once by a wasp and the lady in the kitchen put a bicarbonate paste on my arm to stop the sting. There was a sweet shop across the road which I was in trouble for visiting at a lunchtime once, along with several other children! In the playground, we used to do handstands against the wall, French skipping and sit and play 'jacks'. I remember two particular teachers, their lessons were always fun, and I enjoyed being in those classes. I remember the chess club. I loved that school. My younger sister Clare joined me there when she was about five years old.

Mum, dad, my sisters Jo, and Clare were and always will be my family. That is where my home was, that is where I was brought up. I often thought about the other mother I had been born to, and I suppose at that age I must have been satisfied with the information mum had given me. I had been chosen. I have extraordinarily little memory of life before mum telling me I was adopted, except for kindergarten, I remember the big round white counters and the bourbon biscuits mum wrapped for break time, in grease-proof paper. My memory is prompted by photographs and family stories, though I have few memories of my own.

I do not remember being treated any differently by anyone in my family following that monumental conversation with mum, behind the sitting room door. I think I felt different though, and therefore behaved differently. I seemed to get into trouble more often. I did things that I should not have done. I apparently broke some pieces of Jo's china, dolls tea-set, broke a vase when we were playing in the sitting room, pushed Clare on the swing and kept going even after she asked me to stop. I do not remember deliberately doing these things, though clearly, they happened. Perhaps I was sub-consciously testing relationships. Perhaps I was just being a child. Perhaps I was proving that I was different. I do remember colouring some of our lovely Alice In Wonderland wallpaper in the bedroom that I shared with my younger sister and mum being very cross. I remember staying in our bedroom whilst Jo and Clare went to the circus, I think that may have followed the incident with the vase. Apparently, I denied breaking it when I had been seen. Why? It seems I entered a self-destruct period in my life, and I believe it lasted for several years.

When I was ten, my dad retired from being a veterinary surgeon at the age of forty, and took all the family, five of us in total, on a round-the-world tour together. We lived in close proximity for about seven months. We visited twenty-five countries, stayed with friends, family, camped, travelled by sea, air, train, and in our converted sausage van. The experience brought us closer together, although of course there were moments …. We had so many new experiences, we had tea in a Bedouin tent, having gone off to investigate, and leaving mum to catch us up. The tents, camels and families had set up overnight, not too far from our van. We were invited to visit a Syrian family in their home at the border where we shared sweet tea and unleavened bread. We were gowned in black with shoes off and head coverings on, to visit the Omayad Mosque in Damascus. We rode camels and visited pyramids, dad stood with a tray of leather wallets to sell whilst the vendor went off to find some change in the middle of Cairo, it went on and on with so many memories. We visited countries we had only heard about; some we had never heard of. We learned about and experienced different cultures, religions, and customs. We learned how to communicate when there was no common language. We saw more of dad than we had ever done, he had always worked such long hours, and during this time we were a family, together, and dependent on each other. Mum had to return to the UK for a while as her father was poorly whilst we were travelling through Greece. We continued the trip until she was able to re-join us. Towards the end of the trip dad had to go home as his father had also become very poorly. We said our goodbyes as we boarded the boat for our homeward journey from New Zealand and dad flew home and met us at Liverpool docks about six weeks later. Looking back, I realise that family commitments for mum and dad had at that time been incredibly stressful. We were on the other side of the world and communication was not as easy as it is now, this was in the 1960s. I can remember mum having to go to the local post office to book a telephone call, so that she could return later in the day to call her mum and dad. Dad must have done the same, each was an 'only' child. I remember the blue airmail letters that mum and dad used to write, as we did to grandparents and to dad's aunts. Those seven months we spent together were a truly great adventure, filled with happiness and, I can't help thinking, made me feel much more secure.

On our return Jo, Clare and I began life at our new school in Cornwall. We always said we had moved from Devon to Cornwall, via the world. We became weekly boarders at our new school. Mum and dad seemed to settle very quickly into their new life on the farm and soon made friends with local people. Of course, we then made friends with their respective children. I enjoyed the new school and whilst I always looked forward to the weekends, I enjoyed returning to school on Sunday evenings. I took part in after school activities, netball, tennis, badminton, Red Cross and completed my homework. I played the guitar with friends and listened to music. Happy days.

At weekends I would sometimes stay with a school friend or a friend would come and stay with me, the same for my sisters. We would ride our horses and perhaps help dad with moving sheep. Life was uncomplicated.

When I was twelve years old, Suddenly, a shadow like a huge dark cloud drifted across my seemingly perfect life. I developed what my dad called a 'bark' of a cough, he was a vet after all and likened it to 'kennel cough'. My lips would frequently turn blue and fingers white. It turned out that I had a hole in my heart. Suddenly, the question was there, all the time! 'Has anyone in your family had heart problems?' Mum would answer 'Catherine is adopted, and we know nothing about the family's medical history'. 'Oh, I see!' used to be the standard answer, with the suggestion that this was not at all helpful!

I suspect that all adopted children have fantasies about what their birth mother looked like, what kind of person was she? I had those fantasies about mine. I knew she was an SRN, I imagined her in her uniform, taking care of people, I was never able to give her a face though. Since I have studied a great deal about attachment, separation, fostering and adoption, and have had my own three children, Elaine, Philip and John along with four grandchildren Bethany, Daniel, Matthew and Freddie; I am more able to put my jigsaw together. I realise that the continuing questions about medical issues had triggered something in me, and as a child I had always wanted to know more about my natural mother.

Subconsciously perhaps, I wanted people to know that I was struggling with the whole concept, my anxieties and confusion, along with my lack of understanding was very real. I could not voice or comprehend those feelings and emotions at the time. Hence, I made up my fantasies about why my mother had not been able to keep me. I never thought that it was that she did not want me. Mum had been noticeably clear from that day behind the sitting room door, to explain that my mother, Margaret did what she thought was best for me.

Since then, in a life very involved with children and young people in difficult situations, I have learnt that it is important that adopted children know about their history, culture, and roots. These days adoption preparation is different and more information, family information and life stories are available to the child and the adoptive parent. Where it is appropriate to do so, the natural parent/s are also involved in giving and receiving information. Letter boxes can be set up so that natural parents can keep in touch with their child through birthday and Christmas cards with occasional letters or information that they would like their child to receive when they reach eighteen years of age. Whilst a child may well be in foster care prior to adoption, they may work through a life-story book which may include photographs of their natural parents and perhaps grandparents, and siblings. Treasure boxes are put together with special things that have belonged to the child, or something that the parent would like them to keep, to remember them by. Improvements have been made; lessons have been learned. The 'Quill Box' became my 'treasure box'.

I am aware that my mum and dad went through a rigorous selection and assessment process in preparation to become adoptive parents, though I was shocked at what I considered the laid-back approach shown by the adoption society on having found a possible baby for them. My parents were away on holiday at the time and the letter read:

May 3rd 1956

Dear Mr and Mrs...
I think you are in the middle of your holiday, but I want to tell you about a little girl we have for adoption, in case you feel she might be the right one for you. Her name is Catherine … she was born November 24th and is at present fostered in a very good home in Ilfracombe Devon. Her Mother is a girl of 28, a trained nurse (SRN) the Father is a cable engineer, at present in New Zealand for his firm. Both parents have good backgrounds, with Grammar School education and both come from good homes, the Father on the maternal side being a security officer, and on the paternal side also an engineer.
There is Irish blood on the Father's side; he is tall and fair. The Mother is also rather fair, and tall; they are both musical, and fond of such hobbies as photography, handcrafts, and reading. Catherine is a sweet baby, and although not large, is doing well. Her Mother hoped to keep her but has come to the opinion that for the child's sake she should ask for adoption for her. She is at present working as a mobile nurse in the West Country but will soon be going back to her home county of Cheshire, and later, to South Africa.

If you would like to see Catherine, will you write to her foster Mother, making an appointment to see her? I do not know when you come home again, but if you should feel that Catherine is the right baby for you, it would be in order for you to take her home with you. If you did do that you would remember to notify your Children's Department that you had her, so that your probationary period could start, and please will you let me know too, how you feel and what you propose to do if you want to consider her. My home phone number is… If you want to ring me.

Yours Sincerely...

Now that I have been a Council Foster Carer, among my many other roles. I know that the assessment is a rigorous process these days and that this is now seen as the beginning, not the whole process. The planning that goes into making good placements is time consuming and in most, though not all cases there is an opportunity to get to know the child first. You might begin with a conversation with their present carer or the social worker, you might then meet at the home where the child is placed. Perhaps then take the child out for a visit, progressing to a full day and then an overnight stay. You will be given as much history, on a need-to-know basis from the foster carer or the fostering social worker. In my case these preliminary visits should have happened for all the children I took on placement, and I was a short-time foster carer. I was not looking to adopt. Where the preparation process was rushed the placements were quite often more complex, and then, the child would take more time to settle.

Today the process for adoption is similar to that of fostering, firstly you make an application, then you will be allocated a recruitment officer. You will go through a thorough and very personal, sometimes intrusive assessment, looking at and discussing your own childhood, your deepest thoughts, and fears, along with the practical elements of a tidy house and welcoming home. There will likely be training and other learning opportunities on offer. There would be police checks, and between ten and twelve weekly visits from a social worker and references in respect of your suitability to adopt. This two-stage process takes approximately six months. Following the approval process a report would be submitted to the adoption panel. The panel is likely to be made up of professionals, an adoptive person and possibly an adoptive parent. Once you have been approved to adopt, your agency or local authority would begin to actively match you with a child or children either locally or from out of your area. Whilst this process may change slightly according to your location, it is still rigorous and planned, to give the best possible chance of a successful placement.

I have friends who used to foster babies awaiting adoption. The time and effort that was put into supporting and working with the adoptive parents was amazing, including invitations to spend time at the foster carers home, getting to know the babies and their routine, helping with feeding or bath time. Allowing those prospective adoptive parents to soothe and play with the baby, begin to form a relationship, and really get to know how to respond to their cries and giggles.

We know about the importance of attachment, the physical along with the emotional care and support, the commitment made and given to a baby or child by their main carer. Attachments are usually made within the first few weeks /months of life and usually to the mother as main carer. Where this has happened, the child should be able to make a strong attachment to multiple individuals and even a new main carer. Where these attachments have not been made the child may have real issues and never make strong attachments to their main carer or indeed to other people throughout their lives. It may be that this is the primary reason for the breakdown of some fostering and adoption placements. Knowing this and knowing about attachment theory, is why I was so shocked when over the years I have read and re-read that letter from the adoption agency to my mum and dad.

Mum was a qualified nursery nurse and already had one child, lucky for me she was knowledgeable about babies. If I had been adopted by someone without mum's knowledge and experience, they may not have realised that I still needed attention even though I did not cry for it.

I would say that I have had some attachment issues in my life, particularly when it came to relationships and marriage.

I am not blaming anyone for this, just linking what I know about attachment with what seemed like my inability to make safe, trusting, and long-lasting relationships later in life. I do have an underlying insecurity when I get close to people, which over time seems to cause a destruction of my relationships. I put barriers up and push people away. My attachment to my children is totally different, it is unconditional, they are a part of me, and we had good bonding and attachment when they were babies and children, and this continues now that they are adults, as with my grandchildren.

Today I believe the court order to complete the adoption can be applied for ten weeks after the child has started to live with their new family. For mum and dad, it was a further six months before the court awarded the full adoption, at which point the adoptive parents take on all rights and responsibilities for the child. The natural parents lose their rights and responsibilities through effectively signing over their child. In mum and dad's case, my natural mother struggled with the last-minute decision. Mum had sent photographs of me, to my mother, via the adoption agency and instructed the agency that they were not to send them to her until she had signed the papers. When mum told me this, I felt very cross with her, and she admitted that she had been hard on my mother. The truth though, was that I had been mum and dad's child for three months at that stage, and they did not want to give me up, what a dilemma, I realised what a terribly difficult time this must have been for my natural mother on one hand, and my mum and dad on the other. I also wonder what would have happened if my mother had decided not to sign the papers; would my life have been quite different? Would the attachment I had to my natural mother still have been there?

Following the court hearing 19th October 1956, just under a month before my first birthday; mum and dad received another letter, this time from the Bishop of Exeter. He congratulated them on the court awarding the adoption order to them and said:

'The responsibility for her upbringing now rests with you. What she will most need is to be surrounded by an atmosphere of love, and so protected from a sense of insecurity and fear.

I hope that as soon as the opportunity occurs and long before she is old enough to fully understand, you will begin to explain to her that she in an adopted child. This fact can never be kept a permanent secret.'

He went on to say how important it is that I did not hear about the adoption from anyone else as it would cause a lack of trust and confidence. I would say it would have been catastrophic! So, there it is, the advice given following the court case, which also included reference to my spiritual upbringing, help with education, making sure that mum and dad attended church with me, and arranged my Christening, if I had not already been Christened. Whilst I had not been Christened mum and dad kept the name that my mother had given me. It has always been particularly important to me that my mother named me, and I am profoundly grateful that my original name was kept.

Mum and dad were set adrift at this point, apart from friends and family of course. I wonder if they would have received support from the authorities if they had asked for any. On the issue of attending church, I do not remember going to church with mum and dad very often in those early days Though my younger sister Clare did feature in one of those family stories. On an occasion when the two of us went off to Sunday school, Clare put her collection down her dress and then was jumping around searching in her underwear for it when she needed it! This has become one of those memories that gets passed around in the family!

Chapter 2

Into the Void

At about the time of my heart problems beginning I started to become more aware of an empty space in my life.

The constant reference to family history linked with health took its toll, it made me feel something was missing. I developed an empty place, a void that cried out to be filled with something, but I did not know what. It has stayed with me, not always at the forefront of my life it is true. But ever-present. Though it has not nagged at me so much since I have had my own children. It never affected me daily, though it was there, nagging, and needy, highlighting difference.

Mum and dad offered to help me find out about my mother when I became a teenager. They had realised that this was becoming increasingly important to me, to know who I was, where I came from and perhaps to meet my mother. They also knew that this was no reflection on them as they were my mum and dad, and always would be.

Attached to the offer of help there was however, a word of caution. What if Margaret, my mother had begun a new life, had perhaps married and not told her new husband that she had already had a child out of wedlock? I did not want to ruin her life. She had sacrificed so much for me. My mum knew people who had traced their natural mother and it had sometimes ended in rejection. She did not want that for me. I did not want that. And so, at that stage I did not take any further steps, the point was that I knew I had the offer of help when I was ready in the future.

In 1987 I suffered a mini stroke, a TIA they called it (Transient Ischemic Attack). Hey ho, here we go again with the questions! 'Has anyone in your family suffered from strokes?' 'I don't know I am afraid, I am adopted', I said, almost apologetically. 'Ah, I see!' I realised at this point that it was not only important for me to know my medical history, but also for my children.

At this point the search really started. I wrote to the adoption society to see if they could shed any light on my records. In July 1988 I received a letter saying that the records for 1956 'were very sparse' and 'there is certainly nothing to indicate any medical problems at all in either of your birth parents'. Enclosed was a leaflet explaining how to proceed to obtain my original birth certificate 'which might enable you to trace your birth mother'. This last sentence gave me some hope at last.

Having completed the forms, I sent them off immediately

to access my original birth certificate, as this seemed to be the ideal starting point. With that came an address where Margaret had been working at the time my birth was registered, sadly no other useful information. As I suspected, no father named. The next step was to access my adoption papers, this was the only chance I had of finding out more than I already knew about my mother. I sent off my letter July 1988 and then a month later received confirmation that my documents had been sent to my local Director of Social Services and that I needed to state where, and when, I would like to meet a counsellor to discuss the content.

I was furious, my information had effectively been sent to my boss! I could not access my own information without having a counsellor, why? And, I was particularly annoyed that some counsellor would see my personal information before I did – how was that right? I shelved the idea for nearly ten years, I did not want or need counselling thank you very much! In so many ways my decision was a mistake and one for which I was entirely responsible. One for which I have paid the price.

I applied for a job with NCH Action for Children, a role that became one of three part-time jobs which centred around families, children, and education. Over the next few years, I changed my opinion about how much counselling could help people with a range of different issues. I studied counselling as a module, part of my undertaking to qualify and teach in the further education sector. I had initially thought that I did not need counselling as I did not have anything to discuss with anyone else, especially a stranger. I had made my own choice to research my history. Counselling though, would be a means to an end, simply giving me the chance to find out what I needed to know. What I found was that the counselling module I undertook told me a great deal about myself as well as other people. I found it to be very therapeutic.

Having completed my course, and now qualified with a Cert Ed. to teach in further education; I taught full-time in a local college, my subject being Childcare and Education with school leavers and mature students. As our sessions explored the student's roles, needs and strengths, it also seemed that I learned at least as much about myself, and I came to realise that my own yearning was to find out more about my natural mother

After some thought I decided to contact my previous manager from NCH Action for Children and talked about the counselling aspect, and I asked if she would stand as my counsellor. It had been several years now since we had worked together and so after some consideration it was agreed. We met at her home for between four and six sessions. Perhaps because we had a good relationship at the outset, built on knowledge of each other and trust, the sessions were helpful and cathartic. Never having spoken to anyone in depth about my feelings or how important it was for me to find out about my mother, was itself liberating.

Whilst mum and dad were offering to help me with my search, they were as limited as I was. I did not want to upset them or appear disloyal; they had brought me up and cared for me all my life. All the information had been given to me, my adoption was not discussed often and yet it was open, there were no secrets. I remember once, dad's aunt switching off the television as there was a programme on about adoption. Mum asked her to please switch it back on as there were no secrets about my adoption, and it was healthier to have discussion rather than hide it. Whilst perhaps my grandparents and great aunts found the subject difficult to discuss, I had my family's full support.

It was now ten years (April 1998) after the initial letter that I had received to tell me that, information was sparse and there was no information to suggest that either of my parents had any health issues. My details were with the Director of Social Services, I received the letter saying that my details had been summarised and sent to my appointed counsellor, we could now set a date so that the content of those documents could be shared with me. I was ready. Despite all my misgivings about counselling I was pleased, and I felt more prepared to receive this additional information. What else might I find out about my mother, and in a strange way, about me? The date was set, my counsellor came to my home to share my information. My children were already home from school and my husband home from work, so we went upstairs to have the privacy of my bedroom. I was very anxious. I had always known my mother's name, profession, age when and where I was born, and her hobbies. I had no idea what additional information I could possibly find out and the letter had said that there was no information about health issues for either of my natural parents.

I remember quite clearly sitting on the edge of the bed. One double sided sheet was taken from a folder. Was that it? Had I waited ten years for one sheet of paper? Was that all the information, would there be anything new? A few shocks were in store for me. My counsellor read through the first few lines, things I already knew, my birth date, where I was born, except now I had the full address. Then I heard 'breast fed for two weeks,' and my birth weight (identical to my daughter's birth weight). Why was that such a shock, I knew that my mother had wanted to keep me, why would she not have breast fed, especially given she was a nurse. I was still thinking about this when I heard, 'private foster care'. At three weeks I had been put into foster care and then just six weeks later into a second private foster home. Four months after that I was placed with mum and dad to begin their probationary adoptive period.

This all came as a great shock. I knew that mum, dad, and Jo had collected me from someone who was looking after me, I suppose I never really thought about who that may have been. So many things shot through my mind now. I struggled, not so much to understand it as to empathise with the pain and loss my mother must have felt. Having breast-fed me for two weeks and then perhaps weaned me for a week, presumably knowing at that stage that she had made her decision about my impending adoption. I felt so sorry for her, so emotional. I felt real tension in my throat and a tightness in my chest. I was a mother of three, I could not imagine how hard that decision was for her to make. I considered what I knew about attachment, and bonding, and how interruptions can affect an individual in making good strong relationships, both as children and indeed as adults. I was pleased that my counsellor was with me.

I was a baby who had spent three weeks with my natural mother, followed by two sets of foster carers. My mum and dad were told that they could simply collect me. A six-month-old baby who had had multiple carers and that they had never met before! They knew no more than what was written in that initial letter, no bonding, no introduction. In those days I suppose there was no option if the adoption did not work, and perhaps that is why there were horror stories of children living sad and lonely lives. Mum said that I was a good baby and did not cry very much, could this have been that I had become compliant having had multiple carers in my short life.

I would say that it has taken me years to come to terms with this information and we were only half-way down the first side. I found out that Margaret had been at grammar school until she was seventeen years of age, that she had trained as an SRN, which I knew, and that she had been working as a mobile nurse prior to my birth. She wanted me to be bought up in a Church of England or Non-Conformist family. 'There were no adverse medical conditions reported in your mother or mother's family'. She was fair and well built, her hobbies were listed, and I knew about those. Her own mother had died in 1948 of bronchitis. Her father was a retired security officer.

And that was that! The sum-total of the information about Margaret, my mother, and her life. Looking back there was quite a lot of information there and yet my mind could not shift from the breast-feeding and the amount of moves I had within such a short time in my early life.

But there was another side to this and more surprises, the other side of the document. A complete shock, this gave information about my father. The father I never expected to know anything about. His name had not been on the original birth certificate and no mention apart from what was in the letter that my mum had already given me; his appearance tall and fair, his profession, cable engineer and that he was in New Zealand working when I was born. Suddenly, in front of me I had a name, Thomas, his age, thirty-seven when I was born. A home address: he was Roman Catholic, 'no adverse medical conditions reported in father or father's family' and then:

'Reason for placement for adoption: mother did not intend to marry the putative father. She felt "if the child is adopted, she will have a much better opportunity of having a normal, happy life". She herself could not provide a home and wanted her baby to have love and security.' Such sadness in those last few words.

There were a few addresses for Margaret, though they were work addresses I was told, mostly in the South West, and presumably she did not stay too long in her various roles once her patients recovered from their illnesses. These addresses were forty years out of date by the time I received them and so I was advised that there was no point in writing.

I cannot put into words how I felt, having listened to, and then re-read the information. Naturally, my counsellor discussed a few points and re-iterated how much my mother must have loved me, to go through that grief and loss for the sake of my happiness. I just needed time to process this information and to digest it. More than twenty years later, whilst I am writing this book, and checking through the paperwork, it puts me right back there, sitting on the edge of the bed trying to take it all in.

Being a mother myself I could only begin to imagine what my own mother had been through to give me a better life. I appreciated full well that support for single mothers in the mid-50s was vastly different to how it is now, and the stigma immense. With her own mother already dead, and perhaps only her father still around she may have had very little support. And with her job, little chance of taking care of me herself. Mum told me once that she thought my mother had taken a job in a large house in her capacity of private nurse, soon after I was born, and that when she was needed upstairs the kitchen staff would keep an eye on me, she had tried and realised that it was not going to work in the long run. When I needed her, she could not always be there for me. She did what she thought was best. That is what we do as mothers, isn't it? Though, I am not sure that I would have had her strength to do 'the right thing'.

This was my personal information. It had stirred up so many emotions. It gave me information that would help me in my search. I had a possible address for Thomas, my father, although I was sure he would have moved on by now. I had three possible leads of work addresses for Margaret, my mother, plus the address on the birth certificate. I knew exactly where I was born, in Exeter, now I had a physical place where I had been with my mother.

I received a copy of a letter that my mother had sent to the Adoption Agency on receiving photographs sent to her from my mum, via the adoption agency. The copy was hard to decipher, though I could see her handwriting, her signature and that was important to me. The letter read:

Dear Miss...

Thank you so much for sending the photographs of Catherine. I was really thrilled with them and she certainly looks a picture of happiness. Will you please on my behalf thank her parents. Catherine is one year old on Saturday. I wonder what lies in the year ahead for her.

Yours Sincerely

Margaret...

The address was impossible to read, it could have been Taunton, Cornwall or indeed an address in Wales, and again was probably a temporary work address, so unfortunately no help in my search. A short letter though, and very precious. There is something special about seeing handwriting, it is very personal. How had my mother felt when she saw those photographs? I think it would have been very painful, bittersweet, though clearly, she was pleased to see that I looked well and happy.

So here we are. I knew my mother was called Margaret and my father, Thomas. I am armed with information and my search can begin to unravel the past.

I start with my original birth certificate which I had ordered in February 1998. No mention of my father, whose name I now know is Thomas. Information about where I was born, my name at birth and an address where my mother was living, or working, when she registered my birth on the 12th December, nearly three weeks after my birth. When I was studying at Exeter University 2000, I went to visit St Olaves House, 32, Bartholomew Street East. A lovely Georgian style house sitting behind an historic area with trees and a green, grassy area. I was comforted at the time having seen a physical place where I had been born and where I had spent time with my mother, such a quiet and pretty outlook from the house onto the green.

In 2018 whilst trying to find out the function of St Olaves House, where I was born, I came across this in an article of

Exeter memories, A Lovely Street. written by Mrs FJ S.

"There was St. Olaves House for fallen girls in Bartholomew Street - it was the home where the girls used to go to have their babies. You'd see them looking out of the window and they were a right cheery lot. St. Olaves was 32, Bartholomew Street East and ours was 32 Bartholomew Street West and at times I'd have to take letters addressed to people up there. And this old 'dutch' used to answer the door, a typical matron, starch and cap and face like a wet week".

This short paragraph shocked me and I felt sad that Margaret, who had a profession and was not a 'girl' was in a home for 'fallen girls'. I realised that this was simply an expression, and a label, for women of all ages in my mother's predicament. It saddened me. Of course, I had thought, perhaps hoped, that this was a maternity home, well it was, of a kind. It is strange how written information can have such a powerful impact. I understood about the stigma of being an unmarried mother in the 50s, though I had not expected that. You hear stories of how young, single women were coerced into having their babies adopted or put into children's homes. Is that what happened to Margaret, or did she make the decision herself. Will I ever know the answer?

I have found out through the social-media Exeter Memories group that the mothers from the home were found work in the big houses around Exeter both before and after the birth of their child. I knew that Margaret had worked in a big house, as I mentioned earlier. It seems that the babies were looked after by staff and perhaps some of the other mothers who for whatever reason were not able to work. One person commented that you could see the row of prams lining the drive, as you went past on the bus. Perhaps I was in one of them. I suppose the work in the big houses paid for their keep at the home, which was run by the Church of England nuns from St Winifred's. Many of the babies were then Christened at the Church near St Olaves.

Whilst upsetting I also found this information interesting, especially with reference to my mum saying that I was an easy baby and did not cry much, this was I think due to having become compliant, with multiple carers in a short time. There would have been plenty of mixed messages along with the idea that babies' self-sooth if they are left to cry. Routines would have been strict, for example feeding times, rest and fresh air, some of which resonates with the Norland Nursery Training College where I undertook my own training in the 70s. Compliant babies and children are not always easy to care for, as sometimes they do not react or respond to touch, cuddles or smiles as readily as others. This may have been confusing for my mum who had already had a daughter and had experienced the natural maternal bonding and attachment. My mum had trained as a Norland nursery nurse and would have cared for babies who had had experienced multiple carers, though she also worked in day nurseries.

I wonder now why I had never delved into the function of St Olaves before, perhaps I was not ready. Perhaps I did not really need to know what I now know. That is the thing with research though, the deeper you delve the more complex things can become. And information learned, cannot be unlearned.

At the registration of my birth, the address given for Margaret on the certificate was Grayshott, Hampshire. When I collected my daughter from University at the end of her first term, Christmas 1998 we drove around the area to see if we could find the address on the certificate. Having driven around for some time, not found anything on a map, we arrived at a farm at the end of a long lane and asked the owners if they remembered the property. We were not sure if the name of Nicheley Kennels was the name of the actual property or whether it was a 'kennels', the people seemed rather reserved in their manner when I had explained why I was looking. Perhaps they felt they should not say, or perhaps they did not know. Whilst writing this book, I have of course re-traced my steps, re-visited addresses and previous research. With the internet and media as it is now, I thought I had a better chance of finding out more in 2018, than I did in 1988. So far though Nicheley Kennels does not seem to exist anywhere, even in old records.

In 1998 I hit a brick wall in respect of Margaret's address. In 2018 I have emailed various people connected to boarding kennels, and kennel club in the Grayshott area, perhaps someone will remember something that could at least give me a pointer as to where she was living. I realise that she will no longer be at that address, though it is important to me to know where she lived, somehow it makes her more real, and I feel closer to her. So far, no response.

The other avenue that I had pursued back in April 1998 was writing to the South African High Commission in London. In my adoption papers there had been a comment about Margaret moving to South Africa after she had returned to her home county of Cheshire, following my adoption. I received a letter back saying that they would require the actual date of her birth and the last known address in the UK. Sadly, I did not have this information. I wrote again giving all the information that I did have and again received a response saying that my letter had been referred to the Department of Home Affairs in Pretoria and to rest assured further communication would be sent to me. I have never received any further information and therefore assume that they did not have enough information to continue the search for me.

I did my best to find a birth certificate for Margaret, as I knew this would move my search forward. In those days if the National Statistics office could not find some of the critical information, they did not send out the certificates, they wrote saying that they had refunded the £3.00 per certificate as some of the information given did not match. Now of course, you pay far more to receive the certificate and then find out whether it is a match, you do still receive a part refund if the information is not a match.

During the time I was a lecturer in Child-care at my local

college one of the learning support assistants showed a real interest in family history, she offered to help me. So many people with my mother's initials and same surname. The lady who had offered her help suggested that we could get some details from the medical records from teaching hospitals, it was surprisingly easy to access lists of people who had completed nursing and medical training in Cheshire teaching hospitals. Again, though, we hit a brick wall. Electoral rolls were next and the same situation, no way of knowing which of so many people could possibly be my mother, it was like searching for a needle in a haystack. We received tens of sheets full of people and addresses throughout the UK with the same first name, initial and surname as my mother. We highlighted several that we thought were possible given that people frequently return to their home county and/or to a place where they have been happy.

I have also paid researchers to help with this search for my mother, Margaret. I have a stack of birth certificates that do not quite match in one way or another. I have reams of paper with names and addresses and yet no likely hits, no probable matches at this stage. I am not anxious to throw them away in case I have missed something. One day will something suddenly connect, perhaps.

At one stage I really thought I had found the right birth certificate, the most important points matched. I wrote a letter off to the address I was given by researchers; I was careful to say that I was interested in finding Margaret and sent a stamped-addressed envelope. The envelope was simply so that I knew the letter had been received. Sadly, I heard nothing and did not receive the envelope or any information. On the few occasions when this happened, I would wonder, was that the right address and was it a rejection; I could not let that stop me, I just needed to know, so I would put those experiences to the back of my mind and start all over again.

Chapter 3

From Unknown Relations to Revelations

Following the meeting with my counsellor, I now had details for Thomas, my father. I decided to begin my search for him, as perhaps something would turn up that linked Margaret and Thomas. So, what did I know about him? Well, I had an address and I knew that he was Roman Catholic. In May 1998 I took Philip, my older son up to Scotland to stay and work for a friend who has an estate there. Having checked the location of where Thomas came from, near Liverpool I realised that I would not be more than twenty miles away when coming back down the motorway. So that was my plan. I would visit the town where he came from, starting with the Church graveyard. The town was easy to find as was the church, within minutes I found my father's grave. No, I found a grave with my father's name, a gulp in my throat, I realised that the dates could not be right, he had been thirty-seven when I was born. The grave was likely to be my grandfather, also Thomas. There were other family graves. I was an emotional wreck at this point, all these graves with my father's surname.

The man who looked after the graveyard approached me. He asked if I was alright. Fatal. The floodgates opened. I managed to tell the poor fellow why I was there, he suggested that we go to his office and check the records to see if we could find anything to do with my father, though he was pretty sure there was no grave for him. He was so kind and considerate. Following his search of the lists in his office, he suggested that I went to visit the council office where he thought they may be able to help. Before I left the graveyard, I wrote down the names, and dates of the people I assumed were relatives. I found my way up to the council offices and it was clear that the staff there knew the family. A large family that had remained living in the area over three generations. I was given an address for a probable uncle, possibly grandfather. As I clutched the piece of paper in my hand, I felt like I might finally find one of my parents. On my route out of the town I found the road which had been listed as Thomas' address, I drove along and found the house where he had lived. Suddenly this was becoming very real, perhaps a little frightening. I drove the six-hour journey home with my head spinning, feeling a perfect maelstrom.

Once home, I had to decide what to do with the information I had found. It took me three days to pluck up courage and to think about what I could put in a letter to be addressed to a perfect stranger, and yet perhaps a blood relative, an uncle or grandfather, though I was fairly sure that I had just seen my grandfather's grave.

The content of my letter was as follows:

May 30th, 1998

I have spent three days trying to decide what to put in this letter and decided that honesty is by far the best policy. I am in the process of trying to trace my parents Margaret E.W and Thomas P.

I was adopted as a baby in 1956 and have only recently acquired information I needed to start a search for my natural parents.

My Mother was an SRN who was twenty-eight years old and came from Cheshire. My Father was thirty-seven years old and came from Lancashire. My paternal grandfather was a retired cable engineer, like my father, and on the maternal side my grandfather was a retired security officer. I had this address for my Uncle, or grandfather.

Whilst returning to Cornwall after a few days in Scotland, I decided to call into your town and check out the address in my documents received from the adoption agency. I also decided to visit the Roman Catholic church graveyard as I knew my father to have been Roman Catholic.

The groundsman at the cemetery was extremely kind and helpful. He suggested that my father may have worked for BICC (British Insulated Callender's Cables) and he also told me that you were likely to be a member of the family. He suggested that I visit the registrar of deaths at the council offices, that is where I obtained J's address. I did drive past this address when looking for the other address I had been given, however it did not seem appropriate for me to call in with no warning; it would not have been fair.

I appreciate that this will be a lot to take in, and that you would want proof of my identity – before disclosing any information. I understand that my father was in New Zealand either working, living or both at the time I was born in November 1955. It is thought that my mother was going to continue her nursing career in South Africa.

I understand that it was my mother who made the decision not to marry, even though they were both free to do so. I feel that both my parents had my best interest at heart and made an exceedingly difficult decision to have me adopted. I have three children myself and I could never have found the courage or selflessness to have given them up.

I have had a good life with plenty of opportunity given to me. I am concerned that time is running out for finding my parents, my mother would be about seventy now and my father nearly eighty years of age. I will forward a copy of this letter to the second address that I have been given.

Please acknowledge receipt of this letter if only by returning the stamped-addressed envelope. However, if you can help me in my search please do. I want to know about my family, and I want to be able to tell my mother and father that, my parents, mum and dad have been very good to me, given me experiences, opportunities, a good education and continue to be there for support and help.

Yours Sincerely

Cathy

Three days after sending off those letters I received a telephone call. My letter had been sent to an old address and the person living there had taken it around to where those people now lived. I was speaking to someone from my father's family. I spoke to auntie Lil, she was married to my father's younger brother, and I also spoke to cousin Christine. I could not tell you exactly what we talked about and all these years later how I wish I had written notes at the time. But the amazing thing as I recall it now, was the fact there was no shock or horror that I existed and no scepticism as to who I was. During the conversation I was told that my father had died several years previously, in South Africa. It was strange that no one seemed to know the exact date when he had died.

Suddenly it was all becoming a reality. Since the age of sixteen I had thought about tracing my natural parents and had then put the idea on hold, perhaps scared of rejection. At that point I only had my mother's name, age, and profession to go on. I wonder if I would have found my father before he died, had I started back then.

Auntie Lil had told me over the phone that my father had died many years ago. Having said it, she must have realised what a shock that would have been for me. Immediately she apologised and said she would call me back later when I had had time to absorb what she had said. She was so sorry and felt terrible about the way the information had come out. Apart from registering my father's death, the conversation was like a cloud that lifted and vanished.

I cannot describe the shock, and feelings of grief, and the deep sense of loss that I felt; for someone I had never met, someone who may not even have known of my existence. I had found and lost all in the same moment. And yet I felt that I belonged. I remember going out into the garden as I did not want my children to see how distressed I was. I sat out on the wall, tears fell, sobs came from nowhere and racked my shoulders. It was for the loss of something and someone I had not known. I never expected to feel such sadness and grief. Little did I know that my story had just begun. Over the next few days, I experienced so many conflicting emotions that shook my mind and body, so many thoughts jumbled my mind. I have a family, a different family, one that I had never known.

So where to next? Start with what I know. I am travelling up to Scotland again soon and decide to get together all my relevant documents pertaining to my father, Thomas. I would speak to my auntie Lil and see if it is possible to meet up when I am on my way to collect my son from Scotland. Christine arranged a time, 1pm at Dean's House, and a date in mid-July, just six weeks after our first contact. Expecting to find out loads of information about Thomas I decided to write to the South African High Commission, (it seems he died in South Africa) to see if I could find out whether Margaret had in fact gone to South Africa to work, as it said in my adoption documents; and perhaps even met up with Thomas again. Fairy-tale outcome, well who knows, some dreams come true?

After a six-hour drive, I arrived in the town to meet some of my natural family. That sounded so good. I parked in the same car park I remembered from my last trip. I walked up the street to the Dean's House and up to the door. Ok, now the nerves hit. I hesitated, what if they do not believe me. What if they do not want me in their family. What if, what if, what if? No good, I am here now, what have I got to lose, I walked inside. It was so quiet, hardly anyone there, so I relaxed a bit and walked to the bar and order a fruit juice. Before I had a chance to pay, I heard someone call 'Cath, Cath'. Well, it cannot be me; no-one knows me here. Again, 'Cath, over here'. This time I turned around and saw a small group of people sitting at the back of a large room which I had not noticed when I came in. The pub seemed dark after the bright sunshine. People start waving and calling me over, I looked around to see if it could be for someone else. No. I began to walk over, and a lady stands up and walks towards me. 'Well, there's no denying you' she says.

That was my auntie Betty, she was the youngest of the girls in the family, Thomas' little sister. I was introduced to

40

auntie Lil and auntie Margaret, another of Thomas' sisters. Cousin Christine and her partner John were there. Everyone smiling, open, accepting and commenting on my likeness to cousin Jean who was apparently tall like me and even had the exact same hairstyle at the time. She was unable to come as she, along with many of my twenty-nine cousins was at work. Twenty-nine cousins! And after never even having had one. It may sound ungrateful but I was pleased that so many people were at work! It was quite an afternoon, so many questions on both sides. Did they want to see the documents that I had, 'no, we can see who you are, straight away'. Rather a cliché, but this was quite a surreal experience. I was a part of this family, I was accepted, yet I was a stranger. Everyone had heard about me through the bush telegraph since my letter had arrived and been passed around, and I knew nothing, apart from my brief conversation with auntie Lil and cousin Christine. It would be an understatement to say that I was somewhat over-whelmed by that meeting.

I remember what my auntie Betty said to me during that first meeting. 'You will get to know your father, through knowing the family. He was a very private man and he would have found it difficult if you had come into his life so late on'. I understood what she was saying, as in a way this was what mum had always tried to tell me about finding my mother. I had a feeling that I would get to learn a great deal about Thomas through this family. The first thing being that he was always referred to as Tom by the family and so that is how I shall refer to him from now on.

I stayed the night with friends a few miles up the road, a colleague from my lecturing days, following the get-together, you could not honestly call it a meeting as it was far too raucous. With my head still buzzing and an amazing, new sense of belonging, I had a short drive to my friend's house, and when I arrived, I was able to start processing all the information that I had gleaned from my family. That sounded good, 'my family'. I telephoned mum and dad and told them how it went and what auntie Betty had said about how Thomas (known as Tom to family) may have reacted if I had turned up out of the blue. Indeed, did he even know I existed? The family certainly knew nothing about me, but then auntie Betty had said what a private man he was.

On the way home from Scotland, I told my son Philip all the news and he seemed to share my enthusiasm. We already had a family and now we had a massive extension of family. By the end of July, I had exchanged letters with auntie Lil, and photographs. There was another surprising bit of information that auntie Lil gave me in one of her letters and that was, Tom had been married before I was born, and that I had a half-sister.

I never expected that, I already had Jo and Clare and now a bonus. It seemed that no one in the family knew where she lived, just where her mother had come from. This was something else to investigate, an addition to my list of questions. More questions than answers at this stage that is for sure. Most of the family live quite close and within the same town, certainly the aunts and uncles anyway. There were three aunts and seven uncles on Tom's side, though by the time I met the family there were two aunts and three uncles remaining. And do not forget the twenty-nine cousins!

For the rest of 1998 I did not get to meet up with the family, as I had to have an operation in the September, and prior to that I had arranged to take my children to America. Elaine had taken her A' Levels and was due to start University, Philip had taken his GCSEs and was due to start College and John would be progressing to a Junior class having completed Infant school. My friend Rosy and her husband were posted in Virginia USA and had invited us to take up this wonderful opportunity to spend a fortnight with them and their daughters.

The next get-together was to be during the Easter holidays 1999 so that my children could meet a few members of the family. We had been in contact a great deal though since that first meeting. I had now been introduced to the aunts and uncles along with several cousins through photographs, telephone calls and letters. One of the early photographs that I was given was of my grandmother with Tom, uncle Joseph and uncle Jim. Tom was probably about five at the time, given that Uncle Jim was the baby sat on Nan's knee (everyone called her 'Nan').

When we visited in the spring of 1999, I should not have been surprised that an enormous party had been arranged so that we could meet as many people as possible. I now know that cousin Aggie had been the orchestrator of the party. Once again, I felt very overwhelmed as did my children. However, we had a great deal of fun and chatted to so many people. I wish I could remember everyone who was there and what they said. Auntie Betty kept looking at me and smiling from across the room and when I asked her why, she said, 'it is uncanny how many of Tom's characteristics you have, the way you move your hands when you talk, your smile and other expressions. It is like looking at him sitting there, it makes me happy, makes me smile.' Tom was the eldest boy and Betty the youngest girl, a little bit of hero worship there I believe. My dad would be interested in the similar characteristics as he often talked about which was stronger nature or nurture, perhaps this was nature showing its strength.

Auntie Betty proved to be a bit of a liability, Elaine noticed that she was pouring vodka into my tonic water, lucky we realised in time, and as Elaine had already passed her driving test, she drove us back to where we were staying for the night. I felt fine, though I was unaware of how much vodka I had consumed! Not being a driver, perhaps auntie Betty thought we had organised a taxi to attend the party, I had not even thought about it. Later when I said to auntie Betty about the vodka, she said she thought I might relax a bit more if I had a drink. She was known for her habit of always buying a pint because it was cheaper, though she only ever drank out of a half-pint glass.

I wish that I had spoken to more people, remembered who was who, and connected to whom, and most of all I wish I had asked more questions. One of my uncles, Dan had worked in South Africa with my father and the other, uncle Jim, though I never knew him, had been over for holidays, both had stayed at his house with Tom's second wife, both before, and following Tom's death. I should have asked them where he had lived, what had his address been, where was his place of work. What were his hobbies, how did he spend his leisure time? If only I had asked all the right questions. But at the time I was simply overwhelmed by the novelty of it all.

This was a quick visit and so we did not meet up again after the evening event, although once again plenty of letters, photographs and phone calls were exchanged over the next few months. The family were pleased to have met my children, Tom's grandchildren, and again saw family likenesses, they in turn, took it all in their stride and chatted for most of the journey home. The story of a family I had never known, was unfolding in front of our eyes. It was exciting, and somewhat unsettling, in a good way. We all wanted to know more.

Some of what I had found out was that Tom was a capitalist and most of the family were socialist. Everyone said that Tom was different from the rest of them. Tom left school at thirteen and became an apprentice to a builder, he continued his education through night school. He was not a grammar school boy as the adoption papers suggested. So, he was self-educated. He was a clever man and particularly good at languages, speaking four foreign languages, and excelled at all things related to business. Tom was the first in the street to have a motorbike and between 1946 and 47 he had a bad accident which left him with a scar on the back of his head following hospital treatment. This added to the scar that he already had when he joined the army, apparently from an accident when he was a labourer. He was also the first in the street to have a car, a sports car at that, and he used to take his younger brothers and sisters for a spin. He wore smart suits and was fanatical about fitness. He disapproved of spending leisure time in pubs and made his feelings on the subject quite clear to his siblings as they grew up, he did however enjoy the occasional tipple of whiskey at home with his dad! Tom enjoyed music and singing. The family home had a piano and when the family gathered around, Tom would sing 'Take me home again Kathleen' and 'Danny Boy' amongst other favourite songs.

I suppose that being the eldest of initially eleven children, (sadly one of his brothers, John, died aged a few months) would make you different, for example he was eighteen when auntie Betty was born and twenty when the youngest, uncle Derek was born. When Derek was just six months old Tom had already enlisted with the army to fight in WW2 and became one of the youngest sergeants in the tank regiment.

Tom was always awfully close to his mum and dad, had

tried to help them with his earnings when he could, he was also very close to Joseph, his younger brother by two years and auntie Lil's husband. As the rest of the family were born, Tom would have already been at school. Nevertheless, they were a close family and still are.

Auntie Betty told me about Tom having had a wooden toolbox, everything had its place and was always in its place, he liked things to be just so. She also told me a story about his Errol Flynn moustache, he was immensely proud of it. Once when he was stood in front of the mirror trimming said moustache; auntie Betty being quite young, teasingly told him that he was getting a bald patch on the back of his head, the scissors slipped, and he cut a nick out of his moustache. She said he whipped around so quick she ran out of the room and into the garden. He was not pleased. He was very vain, and now upset! But auntie Betty thought the world of him, he was her hero. Whilst she knew the buttons to press and frequently referred to him as a 'rum-bugger' she loved and admired him, as only a little sister could.

Thanks to all these snip-its, mostly from auntie Betty, I am getting a feel for Tom as a brother and a son, though I will never know him as a father. He had been born and brought up in Merseyside and he had died in South Africa, having lived, and worked there for approximately twenty-five years, he had South African Citizenship. He loved that country and one day I intended to visit and find out why.

Chapter 4

Dunkirk to Nuremburg

In 2000, I contacted the South African Commission Consular Section. I was unable to get anywhere with my mother Margaret's whereabouts as I had no date of birth for her, or a recent address in the UK. Perhaps I could find out more about my father Tom through them. When did he start work in South Africa, how long had he lived there and maybe even an address of where he lived? I have never really had a response, there were details that I did not know and could not give, such as his address in South Africa and date of arrival, his ID number. Twenty years on I am still trying and still waiting!

2001, I tried to access Tom's army records from the Ministry of Defence. The report was sketchy, though it gave an overall of what he had been doing during the war, little detail. He enlisted into the Kings Regiment 15th July 1939 and he was discharged twenty years later from the Reserve

Liability as you can see from the list below. He was part of the British Expeditionary Force (BEF) and he was posted in North West Europe.

Deemed to have been enlisted into The Kings Liverpool Regiment (Army Reserve-Militia) and posted to Depot **15.07.39**

Transferred to Lancashire Fusiliers and posted to 1st Battalion 6th Regiment **20.01.40**

Appointed Lance Corporal **20.09.40**

Posted to Headquarters 125 Infantry Brigade **04.10.40**

Promoted Acting Corporal **08.10.40**

Transferred to Royal Armoured Corps and posted to 10th Armoured Brigade **01.11.41**

Promoted Acting Sergeant **12.06.42**

Posted to No.3 Army Selection Centre **17.04.44**

Posted to Depot **08.06.44**

Posted to Civil Affairs Mobilisation Training Centre **31.03.45**

Permanently attached to Control Commission for Germany **01.04.45**

Posted to No.1 Liaison Unit **14.06.45**

Released to Army Reserve **09.10.46**

Discharged from Reserve Liability **30.06.59**
(Auth: Navy, Army and Air Forces Reserve Act 1959)

Service with Colours **15.07.39 – 08.10.46**

*Overseas Service: British Expeditionary Force (BEF) 1***1.04.40 – 27.05.40**

North West Europe **24.05.45 – 06.08.46**

Tom was appointed Lance Corporal in 1940, promoted to Acting Corporal a month later and Acting Sergeant eighteen months later. I imagine that happened quite often during the war, from enlistment, receiving training and then being allocated posts and position in quick succession. The information also told me some more personal information such as his first wife's name, where they had married and his address on discharge, more leads perhaps, both to Tom and his daughter. Tom was apparently 5'6¾" tall, weighed 131lbs, had grey eyes and brown hair, his chest measurement was 37½", he was Roman Catholic, had a scar on the back of his neck (from the accident whilst labouring). His trade on

Tom (father) enlisted in the King's Liverpool Regiment 1939

enlistment was a brick-layer's labourer. I have a photo of my father which was probably taken soon after he enlisted given to me by auntie Betty.

One of auntie Betty's memories of Tom as a soldier was that he came home once with his uniform torn, wearing only one boot, no hat and very dishevelled. This may well have been following the early evacuations from Dunkirk, when he was part of the BEF. It seems that Tom arrived back in the UK 27th May 1940. The researcher helping me to investigate Tom's army life through Forces War Records says:

It can only be assumed that Tom was part of D Company which had been detached under Captain R.H Pickles on 17.05.1940 …. they had been left in the rear areas for guard duties ….. D Company, along with a lot of the rear-area personnel were withdrawn from Dunkirk Jetty on 27.05.1940 but were heavily engaged in German shore fire and aircraft, 30 men were killed and 130 injured on the ship. The Company landed at Dover the same day most of the men were taken to Aldershot, some were given leave.

The situation in Dunkirk must have been dire for the soldiers awaiting evacuation, suffering from shellshock, fatigue, lack of clean drinking water. The desperation of trying to get out to the rescue boats. The bombing, the stench of burning oil and death. The numbers of men waiting, waiting. We have been given so many vivid pictures of Dunkirk, through film, stories, and books, though it could never really give us the full picture of what those men went through on the beach. The stench, the noise, the silence, the hope, and the fear. Tom was in the second wave of the evacuation; the previous day one thousand three-hundred men had been evacuated from Dunkirk. At this point it was unsure whether the pier would stand up to further evacuation, due to the damage it had received from German aircraft.

Knowing that Tom was involved in the evacuation of Dunkirk adds to the picture of him, the man. What did the experiences of war do to those involved, how did it affect their relationships, how did they manage to put it behind them and return to civilian life after the war? He was one of the lucky ones. He was evacuated from the jetty. He came home.

During the next twelve months Tom spent his time in the UK, he was involved in exercises including 'Bulldog', my understanding is that these were exercises for all of the armed services, and for Tom, it was to do with 'tank' manoeuvres. He was promoted to Lance Corporal, then Acting Corporal. From late in 1941, the Lancashire Fusiliers become109th Regiment RAC (Royal Armoured Corps.) For the first few months the men were involved with both individual and group training. By early 1942 the Armoured Brigade became the Army Tank Brigade and Tom was made Acting Sergeant. Whilst in Carlton, Lindrick, the Brigade was supplying drafts for overseas. In April 1944 Tom was posted to No.3 Centre Army Selection his final posting *prior to being 'posted to the Civil Affairs Mobilisation Training Team, which would train civil servants or civilians in the ethos of setting up civil affairs under a military government'.*

From 01.04.1945 Tom was attached to the Control Commission for Germany

After the defeat of Germany in 1945, the Commission was set up to support the Military Government, which was in place at the time. The Military Government was gradually phased out and the Control Commission took over the role of 'Local Government'. It was responsible for Public Safety, Health, Transport, Housing, and Intelligence. The forward HQ was in Cumberland House, Berlin. Recruits had to be over 21 and were recruited from, Civil Servants the Foreign Office and demobbed Military Personnel. (Tom would have been 27 years old at this stage)

Auntie Betty also told me that Tom was an interpreter for the Nuremburg trials, and this would fit with his appointment to the No. 1 Liaison Unit. During the time that Tom was attached to this Unit, for nearly a year, he was unable to tell his family where he was posted or what he was doing. Part of the unit was involved as an undercover secret police unit, prior to the trials. Being involved in the preparation of the trials and interpreting all the detail, the first to hear about the atrocities, and not being able to discuss it must have taken its toll psychologically. For his family back home, it must have been hard, not knowing where he was, or what he was involved in, and particularly hard for his wife and children.

Recently I have received an official document from South

Africa giving the month and year of my father's death; now I have been able to reapply to the MOD for further information about his army life.

Firstly, I was overcome by seeing his signature and the form that Tom had completed on enlistment, as I have said before it is strange how 'real' handwriting makes a person. It was also interesting to see that Tom, was not the 'perfect' soldier, in that on a few occasions he was in trouble with his commanding officers! Do we all see our father's as perfect role models, I wonder.

The first incident occurred 30th June 1943 in the 'field' when he used insubordinate language to a senior officer. The second, 6th June 1944, the day before his twenty-sixth birthday when he was severely reprimanded for not complying with a direct order given by his CSM. He was absent from the Company between 10.50 and 12.30hrs. The third and final occasion noted was 25th July 1946 when Tom was stationed in Germany, he was accused of:

Masquerading as a Private soldier or civilian Being out of bounds in the Minden CCG (Control Commission Germany) Club Causing a disturbance in the Minden CCG Club

This occasion seems to have been the most serious as he was in 'open arrest pending disposal.' The punishment was awarded 1st August 1946 and he was sent home to the UK from North West Europe 6th August 1946. Tom was then posted to the 'Y' list and then released to 'Z' list with fifty-six days leave. I am still not quite sure what this means in respect of 'Y' and 'Z' lists. Tom apparently never liked the army as he did not like being told what to do, sounds rather familiar! Given Tom's reputation as being 'a bit of a lady's man' one wonders if his masquerading was to see a lady friend. He apparently found women fascinating and loved spending time talking to them, so cousin David tells me.

Within the forces there always has been an extremely strict code of conduct as to who you can mix with socially, and which club you can attend according to rank.

Tom had been in the army for six years; in one particular year he had served one hundred and eighty-one days overseas with only six days leave: and one hundred and fifty-eight days in the UK. Those times were hard for the soldiers, airman and navy as well as for their families back home.

During his last fourteen months attached to the Commission for Germany there was no home leave, it was all very secretive. During the war it was quite right that the rules were strict and therefore perhaps three behavioural issues may not be too bad. To me it makes Tom human and I can certainly identify with having difficulty with rules!

Another side of his records showed several admissions to hospital, Wharncliffe War Hospital Sheffield 4th April 1943, he was then transferred to the Fulford Annex hospital 17th April and discharged 21st April 1943. He was hospitalised again 10th July and discharged 24th August 1943. The following admission was to the Military hospital Catterick

18th February, discharged 21st February 1944. None of these entries say why he was admitted to hospital and as they mostly occurred within the UK, it is difficult to say whether they were 'action' related. A further admission to hospital 9th January to 13th January 1945 and then there was one occasion when Tom was admitted to hospital, he is stated as having been sent to 23rd General Hospital on 25th March 1946, this was in Bad Oeynhausen in Germany, until 7th April 1946, again no specific information attached.

Tom was entitled to wear the Star Ribbon 1939/45, awarded 14th April 1944. He was also awarded the Defence Medal 1939-1945 and the War Medal 1939 - 1945. I have copies of these medals, having applied through the MOD. I am proud of what Tom did in the war.

Within the additional information from the MOD there were six lines of information redacted and I am told that it can be assumed that this is linked to the Nuremburg Trials. According to 'google' there were six interpreters, twelve translators, nine stenographers for each of the four languages, totalling 108 people. Since finding yet another media site I have found out much more about the Control Commission for Germany (CCG) Minden where Tom was based. Headquarters Military Government Regional Bezirk, Minden and Land Lippe (507) were in Minden. The first location being Barkhausan, south of Minden and later to a new location by the river.

The War Crimes Investigation Specialist Pool, later Unit

(BAOR) were at Luisen Strasse, 1, Bad Oeynhausen with three teams (locations unknown) and were reduced to two teams by June 1946 and became War Crimes Group (North West Europe) this fits with Tom's location when admitted to the hospital at Bad Oeynhausen April 1946.

CCG Minden was a particularly important unit and the connections were very specialist areas during the dates that Tom was there. The navy and others were BIG in Intelligence and other secret matters. Much work was undertaken to get big German Industrialists and High-profile Information from East Germany before the Russians could scoop it for themselves. Some matters were very 'James Bond'. Minden was remarkably close to Montgomery's HQ and British HQ at Bad Oeynhausen in 1945. Due to the secrecy and nearness of locations it is likely that Tom was involved in the trial preparations, hence the redacted lines in his Military records.

When Tom was released from the regular army, and prior to working with the Control Commission for Germany he took his army motorbike home with him as he had had it for so long, he considered it his. The army did reclaim it at a later stage!

I am wondering what Tom would have thought about me doing this research and finding out so much personal information about him. What I find now cannot hurt him, and it has been a great help to me. The question is, should I be able to find out all these things. Many people who were involved with the war and various atrocities never spoke of their experiences on coming home. Perhaps it was necessary to detach themselves completely in order to be able to return to normality and civilian life. It may also be that for certain roles within the war and immediately after; that there could have been recriminations for the family.

I cannot even imagine the effect that war-time experiences had on the people involved, only that it must have affected people in some way or another. Tom was only twenty-seven years of age when he signed up for the CCG and for the interpreter role within the Nuremburg trials. Whilst he had his faults, as we all do, I cannot help thinking that he must have been quite a special person. And perhaps now, I understand more about why he could never be tied down, he enjoyed being on the move and living life to the full. I imagine the role of being a father just did not work for him. He had taken on so much responsibility in his younger life as so many of his era had; now it was his time for adventure with no fear of recriminations for his wife, family, and children. Responsibility had been thrust upon him and now he needed his own choice of freedom and lifestyle. Yes, this sounds as if I am making excuses, however from what I have been told about Tom, I can see no other reason why he would have shirked his family responsibilities.

Chapter 5

Memories and Stories

Returning to the personal issues. What I found interesting from reading the army paperwork, is the variation from the adoption papers, sixteen years later. His hair was fair, not brown, well, he had been working abroad quite a lot and so it had probably become bleached with the sun. He was tall, not really, though perhaps in those days he seemed tall. It is the difference in one person's perception over the more clinical approach that the army would have taken. The family says he had blue eyes and the army say grey. My eyes are blue/grey, and my hair was fair, though distinctly grey now, and Tom, so auntie Betty tells me had a redness to his hair. All these details have helped me to visualise Tom, more than just a person in a photograph, and all the photos that I have at this point are in black and white. When someone tells me that I look like someone in the family it gives me a warm glow, particularly when it is my father, and my nan that I apparently look like, along with likeness to some cousins, Jean, in particular. There are strong family traits that many of my cousins have, the blue eyes, the chin, thin lips, and the big toe! I will not go into detail on the latter.

I have tried to visit the family twice a year at least, since our first get-together though frequently it has been more often. I have stayed with my cousin Aggie, one of auntie Betty's daughters when my youngest son John and I have been up to visit. We would go about visiting various members of the family, Aggie introducing us and making sure that I knew who was who. We would visit auntie Lil, Christine, uncle Derek and his wife Margaret, auntie Betty of course and Gerry her husband, and uncle Dan. Uncle Dan had worked for BICC as had many of the family members over the years and he had worked in Cornwall installing overhead cables in the St Austell area and we used to talk about Cornwall and his time working here. I often thought, did we ever pass each other in the street or was he working near the china clay pits when I had my school trip there. He used to ask me to send him postcards of St Austell area when I got home.

Elaine and Philip were both working at this point and so were not able to come with John and me, though they were always interested in the new information and our visits generally. Our visits were frequently during the latter part of the week and always in school holidays, and many of the family would be at work or catching up with other jobs, though at the various parties we would meet up with everyone. Over the years there have been many weddings, and funerals to attend. It is wonderful to be part of such an enormous family, though of course there is sadness with funerals of people I would like to have known better and yet I had at least known for a while. With only one to three years between most of Tom's brothers and sisters there seem to have been many funerals, quite close together. Twenty years on there is only auntie Betty left.

Weddings, significant birthdays, anniversaries, and funerals are always big affairs and it is always wonderful to meet up with family. I still do not know everyone, and I suspect that I never will, though I am beginning to get to know some of the younger generation now. I do feel amazingly comfortable, and part of something that I never expected.

Latterly two of my cousins have been in Cornwall and have either visited or stayed with us, I have enjoyed showing them the county that I was brought up in and where my childhood home was, and where I live. I live in one of the converted barns on what is still the family farm. Dad converted the barns, the one I live in used to be in part, a stable, sheep pens and the kitchen used to house one of the large grain bins. My home is a part of me, my childhood. As my cousin Jean said when she was down a few weeks ago, it is a different world here, being brought up in the countryside on a farm.

It was at my cousin Jean's wedding that I first met my

present husband Ian. Jean's husband Nigel had worked with Ian and lodged with him, when they had both lived in London. He had invited Ian to the wedding as he said Jean's family was so big, he felt he needed more guests. I understand his sentiment!

At their wedding I sat on the table with uncle Peter and uncle Derek, their wives, cousin Christine's daughter Jeanette and her friend. I knew these people, they were family and we had a good chat and a laugh, catching up on family news together. Over the years, uncle Derek and his wife Margaret have given me plenty of information and Derek used to telephone me every now and then for a quick catch up. It was he who told me about the area where Tom had lived in South Africa and where he had worked. Uncle Derek had been a promising young footballer and tried out for Manchester United, until sadly his medical showed epilepsy, it was considered that 'heading' the ball may have been the cause. His career stopped before it had even begun. Uncle Dan was living and working in South Africa, Tom had found him a job when he arrived, though uncle Dan did not stay at that job for long, he went off to find work wherever he decided to stop for a while. He was still in South Africa for about twelve years even after Tom died, and kept in touch with family through letters, several of which I have either copies or the original. By this time uncle Dan was living as an illegal immigrant as he had lost his passport and his papers, his visa had run out years before. These are chatty letters about the country and how much he loved it, about his lodgings and the people who owned it and a few references to Tom and his second wife. Tom kept in touch with uncle Derek, though no letters have come to light. I was told that Tom came home every couple of years to make sure that the family was well and to see his mother and father, their house was always first port of call. Tom worked for BICC in Venezuela, Brazil, Egypt, New Zealand, Kuwait, South America, Ghana and apparently across Africa having finally worked and settled in South Africa.

It seems that Tom's travels gave him some health issues in respect of malaria, which he contracted on several occasions, to the point where he always had to carry a phial of quinine with him. Tom's mother, my Nan, died soon after he started working in South Africa, he had already been travelling for several years. I have photographs of Tom in Cairo, Venezuela and Ghana and one taken of him in

Tom working for BICC in Cairo early 1950s

New Zealand which would have been taken between 1955/57, he worked there for two years which included the time when I was born, with the adoption completing in 1956. It is possible that he did not know of my existence at all, though the adoption papers suggested otherwise. The photograph taken in New Zealand was very precious to auntie Betty and she had kept it in her wallet for years. I believe it was the last photo that she had of Tom. I felt very privileged that she gave it to me and insisted that I kept the original; I sent her a copy as soon as I got home.

What I gather from cousin David is that wherever Tom lived, he would live as a local, he was never aloof or distant from the people he lived and worked with. In South Africa, he did not live as an ex-pat but as an Afrikaner and learned the language, his reason being that he was living and working with the local people and needed to understand their culture and speak the appropriate language. He travelled all over South Africa, having invested a large share into the telecom company there, where he then commissioned BICC to provide the cables. His wife did not travel with him, she had a local lady to help her keep house, and I believe servants, a large house with a pool. Following his death, she sold up and bought a smaller home, before returning to Scotland where she originated from and where she and Tom had lived for a couple of years following their marriage. Tom loved South Africa and lived a successful life there; he invited his brother Joe and wife auntie Lil to go out and live there to work together. They did not like the idea of living as Tom did, having a lady to help and servants in the house or even the idea of servants, and so they stayed in the UK, but they stayed close. Uncle Jim and Tom had a huge argument at one point as when he was staying with Tom, uncle Jim spoke to the servants. This was not allowed and in Tom's mind put the servants in a difficult position as they should be seen and not heard. If spoken to the servant would be in trouble for responding, and rude if they did not.

Tom still had business in the UK and owned several flats in Manchester which he rented out to students, he was something of an entrepreneur and I suppose he wanted to make sure that he had something to fall back on should he ever leave South Africa. He kept his classic car in storage in the UK so that he could have it whenever he was home. From the description, I think it was a 'C' Type Jaguar. As it was, he ended his days in South Africa, dying in 1979, aged just sixty-one from cancer.

Every visit, telephone call or letter gave me little bits of information to add to the picture I have created. There are so many things that I will never know. I am happy with what I do know. As auntie Betty said right at the beginning; I would get to know Tom by knowing the family. Some of the family stories are quite amusing, they all have a great sense of humour, they have a kind and welcoming nature, are bright and worldly.

Cousin Mark was telling me that Tom would ask auntie Betty when she was young, to go and knock on some doors for him, to see if the husbands were in, he would give her sweets for doing so. What is not clear, and perhaps I do not want to know; was this so that he could call on the wives with his black-market goods and use his charm to sell or was it for a different purpose altogether?

I think this is one of my favourite stories. Aggie, aunty Betty and auntie Marg go and visit uncle Derek in hospital, driven there by Ste, Aggie's husband. When they come out Aggie gets auntie Betty in the front seat and straps her in, auntie Marg gets in the back and so does Aggie. Right says Aggie are we ready, auntie Marg and Aggie look up at the same time. Aggie says, I know what you are going to say, right 'everybody out'. They had got into the wrong car, the driver looking rather perplexed, they all got out, bent double with laughing. Their effervescent humour leaving the driver in their wake.

Another story concerns grandad and his lady-friend Annie, quite a 'portly lady' I gather. They went out for their regular drink on a Saturday evening, years after nan passed away; one particular night they missed the last bus home. Grandad flagged down a motorbike with a sidecar and the driver agreed to give them a lift, perhaps he knew them. All was fine until they got home, and Annie was stuck. Well and truly stuck. The sidecar had to be dismantled to get her out. No-one knows whether it survived to carry another passenger in the future.

And again, when uncle Derek was in hospital, Aggie and auntie Marg busy chatting and arriving in the ward asked the nurse what they had done with Mr. Mc as there was a woman in his bed! The nurse said that they were in the women's ward and that they had walked past the men's ward. Too busy chatting as usual.

Recently I had this wonderful email from cousin David, I had sent him a few chapters of this book to make sure that I had not included anything I shouldn't have, and as he is senior cousin it seemed right that he should be my factual editor.

Cath thank you for part one of your book I found it interesting well done look forward to the rest of it.

How are you keeping hope you are well, and Ian, and the family to, we are ok the weather gets us down a bit can't sleep at night. I was interested in the part where you came to the Deans House to meet up with some of the family, they knew you from the start as I did when I first met you. They say you look like Jean I agree you do, though when I first met you, I saw only one person and that was nan, Agnes, it's your style and stance. Cath you have to face it love you are family, no doubts, I don't have any.

Right, there is one thing I don't think I told you about uncle Tom it came to me when I was reading your book. He had very special friend and his name was Tommy he was a little tin soldier Tom had for years. I asked my dad about it and he said he had it from being a boy, he took it everywhere with him. I'll tell you about your dad, uncle Tom came to see me at nan's one Sunday afternoon when he was home, he said to watch my soldier Tommy and he stood him up on the table, then said Tommy fall down and Tommy fell down I was amazed I think I was 5 years old, but I remember that. God that was 65 years ago, ha, then said

Tom stand up, and Tommy stood up, he would not tell me how or why and never did. When I was a bit older and at school in science class, then I found out that with a magnet and some tin you can do a lot, that was my uncle Tom.

Right Cath my love I did enjoy reading your book and I do look forward to the next part. I will keep it to myself until you are ready. I hope you don't mind I transferred it to my flash drive and printed it out, if the printout is not to your liking, I will shred it.

I look forward to seeing you again in September but bring a birthday card its my birthday ha ha ha ha ha!

Take care give all my best wishes to Ian and the family.

David j 🙂 *keep smiling*

I really wanted to include this email as it gave me such a warm glow when I received it, not to do with my book, but the chat, the reference to Tom and the references to me being like my nan and like Jean. Naturally I asked cousin David's permission, before including it here.

Given the help and support that I have had from various social media pages, I have been able to find a previous address for my father's second wife. I wrote to the address and miraculously received a telephone call from the lady who now lives at the address. She very kindly gave me the name of Tom's wife's niece who I managed to contact. Sadly, I did not get very far except to find out that his wife had moved from her home due to dementia and is now in a nursing home. There are so many things that she would be able to tell me, if her past memory is still intact, though in her condition it may be inappropriate. I must remind myself that Tom may not have known about my existence and that his wife may be totally in the dark. I need to be constantly aware of the impact of my research and investigation on other people.

It took me twenty years to be able to find my half-sister Sue, she too was trying to trace her father. It turns out that she knew even less than I did about him, despite his being married to her mother. That is what the war years did to families. What we have found though, is, having researched his military record it seems he was rarely at home, given his role with the Commission for German and previous postings. I also have a half-brother, Stewart, who I have not yet met, this surprise came out of my first meeting with Sue. Since then, we have seen each other and kept in touch via email and text. We met up, with our respective husbands before Christmas for lunch, though not last year of course due to the pandemic.

Early this summer we had a family get-together here in Cornwall, my cousin Jean and her husband came to stay, we found that there was another distant cousin living in Cornwall, so both she and her husband also came. Sue came with her husband. My own children, grand-children and my sister Clare popped in during the day to say hello. We had a lovely day chatting, finding out and sharing information between ourselves about the family stories and ancestry. Thankfully, cousin Jean was able to furnish us with some stories and we had brought some photos to share between us. Cousin Aggie had given me lots of photographs when I first met her and so I took some of those, along with the ones that auntie Betty had given me of Tom, so many years ago. I really feel like I am putting the bones on all the information gathered over the years. I feel very lucky to have had this opportunity, it makes me feel complete.

Sue is looking forward to coming with me on a future visit to the family, so that she too can meet some of the cousins and begin to know the family. Though our plans have changed somewhat due to the sad death of auntie Betty, the last of Tom' siblings in June (2018).

Aggie telephoned me on Sunday morning to say that auntie Betty had taken a turn for the worse, she was in hospital and extremely ill. She had been poorly for some time, though she had always seemed to find enough strength to get better again despite having problems with early onset of dementia and COPD (Chronic Obstructive Pulmonary Disease) no doubt aggravated by years of smoking.

And so, Monday morning June 4th, 2018, I made a very emotional drive up to visit her. I left home at six-thirty in the morning with the intention of arriving at the hospital by twelve-thirty. I sailed along happily stopping briefly at Taunton Services and then filled up with fuel just before Gloucester. Off I went again until the engine started to 'pink'.

Half a mile and I pulled over to the hard shoulder and immediately checked my invoice. I knew what I had done, again! I had put petrol in my diesel engine. As the RAC man said no one breaks down when they have plenty of time on their hands. Approximately two hours later I was on the move again and the traffic though slow was not too bad. My timing was now completely out. I arrived at the hospital at three-forty-five. Sadly, too late for auntie Betty to hear me, though I took the opportunity to say my goodbye. Aggie said that auntie Betty would have been 'made-up' that I came to see her and said goodbye privately, in her hospital room. Such a sad day. A lovely lady who has, over the years made me a part of this family, has given me information, stories, memories, photographs and has, as she said she would, helped me to know my father. She opened her arms to me the first time I met her, welcomed me, with no questions or expectations. We came to know each other very well and kept in contact for the last twenty years. Through her jokes, stories, antics as the youngest sister she helped me to get to know her eldest brother, my father, Tom. Aunty Betty was the last of Tom' siblings, this was the end of an era. And so now, we, the cousins become the older generation.

Grief is a very selfish emotion. Auntie Betty is in a better place, her quality of life had been diminished over the last five years. She was a great mother, grand-mother, aunt, and friend to so many, we should not mourn our loss, but celebrate her life. I remember asking auntie Betty to come down to Cornwall for a holiday and she said, I worked in Germany once, this is where I live now, why would I want to go anywhere else. She loved her hometown, it had all her friends, her family, and her life. She had been in the Princess Alexandra Nursing Corps in Germany and had really enjoyed her time there, though rarely spoke of it, once it was done, it was done. Auntie Betty did one day as a 'clippie' on the buses, though she lost the bus and the takings were stolen, so there was no second day.

I stayed for a few days and visited Aggie. She was so close to her mum along with her twin sister and two brothers. Auntie Betty had an amazing send off with about twenty people surrounding her in her hospital side-ward, her children and all her grand-children. As my son John said, 'what a way to go!' The funeral took place about a fortnight later and Ian and I travelled up and stayed for a few days. Aggie's daughter, surrounded by the rest of the grand children read a fitting and amusing eulogy, a great tribute to auntie Betty, loved by all. I particularly loved the bit that said:

'She attended Our Lady's School; she left school at 14 years and met the love of her life 'ciggys' (cigarettes). Nan went off to work for BICC, as did most of the family, it was there that she met her future husband, Gerry. 'They say that opposites attract and that couldn't be truer for them, they complimented each other and by that we mean grandad was the calm after the storm nan had created.' Nan was fiercely protective of all her family and whenever a new grandchild was imminent, she would camp out

at the hospital waiting for news and to know that all was well, before going off to the nearest pub to celebrate the safe arrival, usually the Green Dragon.

Auntie Bet was given a wonderful send off by family and friends, with a lovely tribute through the eulogy. The end of an era, a sad farewell.

I visited auntie Marg and also cousin David whom I have not met for several years, though we have emailed and spoken. David gave me some information about Tom, and he said that his first port of call was always to his parent's home, he said that he was a 'lovely, lovely man'. He was awfully close to his parents. After his mother died, Tom would make sure that his father always had what he needed. Uncle Derek and auntie Marg lived with granddad for a while and Tom would say right what can I do to help financially? Auntie Marg says Tom was always very pleasant and his intention was always good, though he rarely remembered to send any money through. What he did do was bought his dad a parrot, an African Grey sent over from South Africa. When uncle Dan returned from one of his overseas jobs, or perhaps it was from Cornwall, uncle Derek and auntie Marg moved out of grandad's house as they had their first baby by then. Uncle Dan moved in with grandad and taught the parrot to swear like a trooper! It was called Mike and used to say 'Dan, Dan, bugger off' amongst other little niceties. Grandad was frequently bitten by Mike, he had a shaky hand due to a war injury to his arm and every time he fed the parrot it would bite him, the more his hand shook the more the parrot would bite. The parrot was also jealous of the new baby, Uncle Derek and auntie Marg's son Michael, and would try to claw him if it managed to escape the cage. I am not sure how Mike got on with grandad's big mongrel dog Rex. Grandad took Rex on many a walk. Rex knew his way to the pub and generally set off in that direction!

There was a time when grandad decided to move out of his house as he and uncle Dan constantly argued. He came around to auntie Marg's and said, that is it I am leaving, moving out. And to show how serious he was he pulled his shaving gear along with his pension book from his pocket. He stayed for a night or two and then returned home after uncle Derek had strong words with uncle Dan. The family were all remarkably close, though could be somewhat volatile at times. With so many of them, that is no surprise. They all looked after each other and moved in and out of each other's houses for times when it was necessary to support each other. Grandad kept chickens at one point and would wring their necks and give them to the family sometimes for their Sunday lunch and as his daughter, auntie Margaret was walking down the street with hers it started squawking and she almost dropped the bag.

When Tom and his wife came home from South Africa for visits, they sometimes stayed with uncle Frank, and auntie Jean, cousin Jean and Anne's mum and dad. Jean says that Tom liked everything to be 'just so' and would get annoyed with his wife if the table was not laid properly or if she had not dressed appropriately for dinner and on one occasion uncle Frank had words with Tom over the way in which he spoke to her. It seemed that whilst they were close and would always help each other out, they were not afraid to tell each other what they thought. Tom's wife has always been described as a 'lady' and was liked by many of the family. Frank would not have Tom speaking to her that way, not under his roof.

There are many more stories of late-night sessions with cousins Aggie and Mark amongst others; staying up chatting until all hours and then Aggie complaining to auntie Marg that the wine was terrible! A family of straight talkers, fierce loyalties, welcoming and supportive to everyone.

I feel like I am coming to the end of this very personal, emotional, and amazing journey. It will not stop, though it

**My paternal grand-
parents Thomas
and Agnes**

has come to the end of an era with the loss of auntie Betty. I will still make my visits and keep in contact with cousins and their children. Social media has helped with choices of how to keep in touch, and see what people are sharing and doing with their lives. I feel, very much a part of this family, and will enjoy getting to know some of the younger generation better. Aggie and I keep in touch regularly and she is a mine of information, having a great memory and interest in family history. I am sure that many more stories will come to light. I hope that Sue will feel as if she has also come to know our dad better and will in time come to know some of the cousins as I do.

So, Tom, I feel like I know quite a lot about you now and that has made me feel more secure, it has helped to fill that void. I could not tell you, any more than I could tell Margaret that I have had a good life, though perhaps you will already know.

Margaret, my mother would be at least ninety years of age now and it seems that after thirty years of attempting to trace her, and a lifetime of wanting to know more about her and what she looked like and whether she went on to have more family, I must draw a line.

My biggest wish has always been that I would get to tell her that I understood why I was adopted and that I had a good life. Who knows perhaps someone will read this book and know whom I am referring to; if so, please grant my wish and tell her what I have said?

Chapter 6

Light at the End of the Tunnel?

After a few false starts, information from a lady who now lives in my step-mother's old house in Scotland; and having researched a list of thirty-one nursing homes in the area; through google earth, electoral roll and the 192 facility, I have finally found an address and phone number for someone who can give me some information about Tom's wife.

I passed the information to Sue as she is Tom's legitimate daughter and therefore his wife, Isabella's, stepdaughter and closest next of kin. Whilst I am Tom's daughter by blood, both Tom and my mother Margaret had given up their parental responsibility for me through the adoption procedure. It is likely that our stepmother would be aware of Tom's children from his first marriage, though he may not have mentioned my existence at all, he was working in New Zealand when I was born, and unless he and my mother were still in contact, it is possible that he may never have known that he had another daughter. Tom did not return to the UK until 1957 by which time the adoption was completed, and I had a new mum and dad. In those days, fathers had no say in whether a child should or could be adopted, it was purely the responsibility and choice of the mother, in the case of an unmarried mother that is.

Sue phoned our new contact the next morning and had a satisfying conversation, explaining who she was and that we wanted to meet our stepmother and were keen to know how she was health-wise. The person kindly told Sue where Isabella, Tom's wife was living. The next thing was for Sue to write to her and introduce herself and of course she also wrote to and then spoke to the manager of the home to explain the situation. At this stage, there had been no mention of me, we were both aware of Isabella's position and wanted to take things slowly. Ideally, we would like to know about her life with Tom, find out more about his personality and give us both some closure.

Cousins Jean and Anne were extremely excited as they knew Isabella well when they were children, and she stayed with them when she returned from South Africa, years after Tom's death. When I contacted them to say that we had found her, Anne could not contain herself and telephoned her immediately. Anne said she sounds exactly as she did years ago and still had a sense of humour, saying that she could still run faster than anyone else. Anne was now going to write and then both she and Jean will visit in September and possibly I would be there as well as I am planning a visit to their hometown, at that time.

I was feeling excited and a little anxious, new leads do that to me. I never know how people will react to me or what impact my arrival will have on them. I have never wanted to cause upset to anyone on this journey and so far, the responses from people have been over-whelming in a most positive way. I have booked the flights and one night's accommodation for Sue and me to go and visit our stepmother at her care home. We have been told that we are able to visit at any time and do not have to make an appointment. I am hoping that we will visit in the morning and then perhaps again late afternoon as that will give us all time to think and digest, and will perhaps help her place us for future contact by letter or phone.

In the middle of all this excitement my daughter Elaine has been chasing up information and leads about my mother. She has found a Cheshire social media site that is helping people find lost family members. My mother would be ninety years of age now, the same as my stepmother and so once again time is against us.

Suddenly everything is moving extremely fast. Elaine thinks she has managed to find my mother's nursing registration number which may well help us move on, she has also found an address from many years ago, you never know though, families sometimes stay in the area. And next week I am going to meet my stepmother, my father's wife, in

Scotland.

I spent several hours on Ancestry yesterday trying to locate information about my mother's date of birth, I became quite excited at one stage as I found information linked to the General Nursing and Midwifery Council and around Liverpool area including registrations from Royal Infirmary Liverpool and University College London, the latter probably incorrect, but you never know. So many people with the same name as my mother and born around 1928, which we think was her year of birth.

It is so easy to become addicted to searching, and to get excited about information; sadly, though, until we can confirm a date of birth, we are simply guessing and achieving little. I came across fifteen thousand entries on ancestry for people with the same name as my mother.

Right now, I am feeling frustrated that I am unable to pinpoint just one of these ladies as my mother. Having recently had a conversation about adoption in this day and age, it is heartening to hear how differently the process is handled now, and how much information is shared, and will be available to the child if and when they decide that they would like to know their history. And I reiterate, that wanting to know about your roots, is absolutely no reflection on the people who have brought you up as their own child, given you their name, your home, and education. Not for everyone, though for some people, adoption leaves a void that can only be filled by knowledge of your past. A need to know where you came from.

With Elaine's help I have found out more about St Olaves, where I was born, and also through a social media page I have found out about other organisations that helped people who may have been in trouble, particularly young girls in Exeter. St Olaves, at the time I was born, was however, for maternity and single mother situations only. It seems that the Devon Archives/Heritage site hold some minute books and whilst you cannot look for yourself due to data protection. In some cases, they can look for you and give you what information there may be, about your own circumstances. It turned out that the minute books contained financial information more than any information about intake, and certainly no individual names are recorded. The Archivist did however send me a leaflet that explained the history of St Olaves, which I have been able to pass on to other individuals who had an interest. Since I began my research, I have been approached by about six people whose mothers were at St Olaves.

I can feel a visit to Exeter, at least for photographs of St Olaves and perhaps to the Archives and as Elaine said, perhaps a visit to the records office in London. Elaine has also emailed various hospital groups to see if we can confirm a date of birth for the nursing registration number she has located.

I am feeling quite heady now as people have also offered help to access my father's death records direct from the Home

Office in Pretoria. My head is spinning with information, excitement, anticipation, and hope, along with frustration over the dead ends. The generosity of individuals continues to astound me. This week I have spoken to a lady whose story was featured on the ITV programme 'Long Lost Family'. She too was born at St Olaves, though ten years after me. We are hoping to meet up at the end of the summer to exchange stories and information, thanks to the programme she has found her mother's family. I am so pleased for her. I did apply to the programme once, though I was not selected and even when I had sent off the application decided that I would find that process exceedingly difficult to cope with. It was at this point that I decided to have my DNA tested to see if there was any chance at all that someone else may have connections to my mother and be a member on Ancestry. There are so many amazing sites that can help with finding family and Elaine and I have used different ones for different information and purpose.

Tomorrow is the day that my half sister Sue and I meet Isabella, the lady that our father married in 1958, the lady that he shared his life with, in South Africa. It has taken time and ingenuity to find her and we have been lucky. Already I feel that we should have organised a longer trip, we are staying one night and will only be able to visit for a couple of hours.

We had not given a date for our visit. I hope that she will want to talk to us and hope that she will want to talk about the family and her life with our father. For me, I am pleased to be meeting the lady that I have heard so much about from family, the lady who made my father happy. There are so many things I would like to know, what kind of man was he as a husband, what did they enjoy doing together. What was it like to live in a country so different from our own, what were his strengths and weaknesses, who was he, really? I would also like to know where they lived and where my father's remains lie.

I know so much about my father from his family. I have heard both good, mostly good, and some not so good aspects of his character which have emerged from this search. He was human as we all are, he had his faults, as we all do. What are the genetic ties that hold us together, I know that I have similarities to him in looks, as the family genes are strong, what about my character, how like him, am I?

I doubt that we will come home with a mass of information after our visit, though I hope it will be the first of many, though being aware of the passage of time. I hope that our visit will revive memories of Tom that may have faded for Isabella. I am taking photographs of the family members that she knew well in the hope of reviving some of those lost memories. Apart from what I need for myself and what Sue needs, I feel that this is something that we can do for our father; he died aged sixty-one years of age, leaving her a widow at fifty-one years of age. Having reached my sixties, I realise how young she was, to live the remaining years of her life alone. Perhaps we can all gain something from this meeting, I hope so.

Sue and I met up at the Exeter and travelled together to Bristol Airport and then flew to Scotland. We stayed at a hotel a couple of miles from Isabella's care home and visited her the next morning. Sadly, her memory was fleeting and whilst she seemed happy to have visitors and greeted us enthusiastically, she seemed confused as to why we were there. We explained who we were and that we were interested in the life that she had shared with our father. She seemed pleased that she had acquired two stepdaughters though she was confused as to why it had taken us so long to find her, she said at ninety years old it was quite a surprise, though it seemed to give her pleasure.

We talked a lot about Tom to her and she remembered who he worked for and what BICC stood for, we were surprised, and she said she had heard it every day of her life with Tom. She said that they had had a wonderful life in South Africa and that she loved Tom very much, 'he was my everything', she said. One of the staff from the home went and found a photograph album belonging to her, there were a lot of photos, though no-one that we recognised, except for one, and Isabella struggled to remember. Coming across a photograph of a house, she said that it was familiar, both Sue and I looked at the photograph and on the back was written, Observatory, in capital letters, I thought it meant the type of building and could not work out why as it was clearly a house. Isabella took it back and then she noticed that there was an address on the back, that brought it back for her, it was the house that they shared in Observatory, a suburb of Kensington South Africa; in pencil, there was an address, which Sue and I had not noticed. The other photo was a lovely picture of her and Tom having a get-together at their house. I said, well that must be Tom and she said, 'well it must be, as I am sitting on his knee, I don't usually do that sort of thing!' I was delighted as I now had their address, which may help me find out more about Tom and his life in South Africa as well as a colour photograph of Tom and Isabella.

Tom and Isabella's home in Klip Street 1960s

Sue and I had so many questions we would like to have asked, though the connections were just not there for our lovely stepmother today, another day it may be better. I asked if she would mind me taking a photograph of her, as so many of the family had wanted to know how she was, she had been well liked by everyone. She was happy to oblige, so long as we gave her time to put her make-up on. We had been with her for an hour at this point and rather than wear her out, we decided to go out and leave her to have her lunch and a rest and would return in a couple of hours.

On our return, she had her make-up on along with her jewellery and did remember us from the morning visit. She said she thought that she knew me, and I said I thought it was the family genes, and I have similarities to several members of the family, including Tom. Looking at the colour photo that she had, the first colour photo I have ever seen of Tom, I am more like my father than I had realised, perhaps, I hope, she saw him in me. We spent an hour with her in the afternoon and took a couple of photographs which she seemed pleased with. We covered some of the same ground as the morning and some aspects seemed clearer for her and she was still very enthusiastic about having two stepdaughters.

Sue and Isabella had both been company secretaries in their work life and she was recounting where all the keys of the typewriter were, given one now, I think she would still be able to type very well. It is amazing what information the brain holds and how it compartmentalises things. She is forthright and on a couple of occasions, said 'who are you, and why are you here' adding that she was happy to see us, just a little confused. She seemed genuinely happy to have two stepdaughters, though still wondered why it had taken so long to find her! 'I am ninety you know', she said on more than one occasion.

We were, I suppose disappointed at not being able to have flowing conversations in order to find out more about their life together, though it was a real pleasure to meet our father's wife, it was an important connection for us. I think she had, and still has a great sense of humour, she is direct, and feisty and I imagine was a good match for Tom, it is good to hear from her that they had a good life together. There was no mention of Tom having died and so we decided it was not fair to raise the subject as it may have caused sadness or confusion, or equally may not have registered. We felt that no one would gain anything from it and therefore it should be left unsaid. I was sorry that she did not recognise family members from the photographs that I took for her and felt it was sad that she did not recognise Tom either, though he is clearly remembered in her mind. I left the photos with her, you never know, on another day, she may remember. One of the photos of Tom, Isabella said if we could take his hat off, she might recognise him.

I have written a letter today and enclosed a copy of the photographs we took of her with her two stepdaughters, perhaps she will remember our visit, I hope so. I shall keep in touch with a card every now and again and when I am up in the area, I will call in again to see her. She may not know me, though I am pleased to say that I have known her.

The other side of this trip was that Sue and I had quality time to spend together, get to know each other, plenty of chat and plenty of questions. We may not have come home with all the answers, though we came home with new knowledge and information that may prove useful in our search. I am going to write to the residents of the house where Tom and Isabella lived in the hope that I can find more clues as to his life in South Africa.

Chapter 7

But for the Price of a Stamp

Sometimes we can read so much that we miss the blindingly obvious!

On my adoption papers that I was given twenty years ago, I had two addresses believed to be temporary work addresses for my mother. As so many years, forty-three to be precise, had already passed, I did not write to these addresses. I assumed that no one would remember the kind nurse who had perhaps looked after a parent or other relative. Also, the social worker who sent the information through said that they were temporary work addresses and that no one would know of my mother now.

A few weeks ago, when going through all the paperwork again with Elaine, she said 'have you written to these addresses', 'no', I said explaining why I had not done so. Well, what have you got to lose she says and so I wrote to both addresses, and to the two foster parents who had looked after me for some time prior to my adoption placement. Having put the letters in the post I walked away and forgot all about it, as I had not expected any response.

It had been a stressful week and following certain circumstances. I had taken my youngest son John to Newlyn, near Penzance to collect a new, second-hand car on Thursday 13th September. When I arrived home, there was some post on the chair and I looked at it, thinking, I wonder what that is. I opened the envelope, a large white A4 and written across the top in bold red pen. Photo–Do-Not-Bend. I took out a photograph of a young women, a nurse, and thought, what is this all about. I looked at the writing on the mask and it said a name I did not recognise. The photograph was beautiful, an official photograph of a lady in her nurse's uniform proudly displaying her Nursing Prize Medal.

There was a letter. As I began to read the enclosed correspondence, I realised that the woman in the photograph was my mother. I read the letter with tears running down my face, struggling to read the print through the tears and sobs that threatened to remove the ink.

John walked in and put his arms around me, not knowing what was happening. It took a while to be able to explain what the letter was about, in fact I just showed him the photograph, and said 'that is my mother, she is dead'.

The letter was in response to one of the three letters that Elaine had suggested I should write. The address, in Stockport was the family home of my mother's first cousin and where my mother had spent much of her time, both before and following the death of her own mother and her grandparents. The cousins had been bought up like sisters and were awfully close. My mother had been born in Colwyn Bay, North Wales, and at the age of three when her own mother became poorly with MS (Multiple Sclerosis), she and her parents moved to her grand-parent's house. My mother's 1st cousin, Edna's parents married and lived in Stockport, Edna was born nine years after my mother.

There were a couple of smaller photographs in a separate envelope and these were of Edna, her mother, and my mother Margaret. Edna's mother was also called Margaret and was a sister to my grandmother who had been called Catherine, Kitty for short. I was delighted to know that I had been named after my grandmother and I had always known that my mother had named me, mum always told me so. To find out why I was named Catherine, was so very special.

It seemed that my mother must have met my father when she was nursing at the Chester Royal Infirmary between 1952 and 1955. On the back of the official photograph, it had been dated 6th June 1955. My mother was expecting me when that picture was taken, and she was looking healthy and happy. Having completed her additional training to gain her SRN (State Registered Nurse) qualification my mother told the family that she had decided to have a change from hospital nursing and was going to work for an agency, BNA British Nursing Association and was off to the South West to work.

At this stage no one knew that she was already carrying her child, me.

The letter went on to say that, it was with great sorrow to my mother that she could not keep me, not because of the situation of being an unmarried mother, more the logistics and practicalities, as at that time other family members were unwell and older, also a lack of space. This bore out what I had always been told that my mother had desperately wanted to keep me. As a mother, I find it hard to even think about what she must have felt, the hurt and desperation must have been unbearable. I can only imagine how hard it must have been for her, and specifically at that time, when there was such a stigma attached to being unmarried and expecting a child. The pain of having to go to St. Olaves for me to be born, a home for 'fallen girls'; so far away from home, and to spend those three precious weeks with me and then to have to say goodbye.

This letter was a bittersweet revelation, I was so happy and yet so sad. Once again, I had found and lost in the same moment. The envelope also contained the funeral 'order of service' for my mother.

I was feeling deeply sorry for myself; I was cross that I had not written to those addresses all those years ago. I was cross that I had been visiting Exeter every week for five years when I was working through my Masters at the University and my mother was living there. I was just very, very cross. If I could have kicked myself, I probably would have! My mother had moved to Exeter around 1967 to become Assistant Matron and then Matron at a new Nursing Home and I could have known her, but for the price of a stamp. Exeter had been her home for forty-seven years, and I live just one and a half hours away, frequently visiting Exeter to see friends, to study and to shop with my granddaughter. I felt angry and empty.

I rang Elaine and told her the news, and in the evening took the letter and photographs over to show Philip, whose eyes filled with tears as Elaine and John's had, at the thought of all those years searching, and arriving at the end, too late to know my mother, their grandmother. I have no doubt that she would have been so proud of her grandchildren and indeed, great grandchildren.

So, this is my mother's story. Having left school, my mother worked in a 'ladies outfitters', good quality clothes and she thoroughly enjoyed the job. Her mother, my grandmother was very disabled with MS (Multiple Sclerosis) and following the death of her mother in 1948 and her grandparents in 1950, she decided to enrol to do her nurse training. In 1955 she was awarded the Nursing medal for being the best nurse in her cohort, she had completed her SRN and her staff nurse training. At this point she found herself expecting me, her baby. We do not know exactly what happened between my mother and father, it seems that my mother had called off the relationship at one point, though it began again not long after; it then finished again, perhaps prior to my mother finding herself pregnant. I still have no idea whether my father knew that she was expecting his baby. Given that my father's details appear on the adoption papers I had always assumed that he knew, now I am not so sure. Either way, he would have had no choice as regards the adoption going ahead. I know that my mother wanted to keep me. Edna told me that my mother, having written to her aunt, and to her father realised that it was not possible to keep me. She did not have her own home. To have gone through the pregnancy and the birth at St Olaves, and then to find that she was going to have to give me up for adoption must have been unbearably hard for her. It shows her strength of character and her thoughts about what was going to be best for me.

My grandfather had turned up unexpectedly to visit my mother's aunt, Edna's mother. This was after they had both received letters from my mother about my birth. The latter to my mother's aunt began, 'have a glass of brandy and sit down, I have something to tell you ......' It seems that my mother went home to Stockport for a few days shortly after having sent the letters. It was around Edna's birthday and when possible, my mother would always visit to be there to celebrate together. Following further conversation with her aunt during her stay, and perhaps her father, my mother, it seemed, realised that she was going to have to let me go and by that stage I was already living with mum, dad and my sister Jo. She went to the adoption office in Stockport and signed the adoption papers. I can only surmise how hard this must have been for her, as my mum told me that at the last minute, my mother had delayed signing the papers. The date they were finally signed was 25th August 1956. Edna's birthday is August 24th. I had been placed with my, soon to be adoptive parents 26th May 1956. I had not known that the papers were signed in Stockport, though of course now I understand, Stockport was my mother's home address and as so many of her work addresses were temporary, of course she would have given the agency her home address.

Literally days after receiving Edna's package in the post I also received the original court papers of the adoption. The information all suddenly made sense. If only this important information had been included in my 'summarized notes' from the social worker. Perhaps I was only allowed it now as my mother had passed away, due to data protection. There was no date of birth for her and no county of birth. Everything seemed to match with what was in the precis version of my adoption papers except that according to the health and welfare checks made, I was not breast fed, and was brought up on the bottle. In so many ways that makes more sense, given the way the routines ran at St Olaves House, I had wondered how my mother would have managed. Had I found that out before contacting Edna, I think I would have been very upset, though now, it makes sense and is more easily accepted. I suspect an error was made when copying information and therefore not a major issue now. It maybe that I was breast fed for the first few days, though I have a feeling that this would not have been encouraged given that most babies were to be adopted. I also have the feeling though, that if my mother thought that was the right thing to do, she would have done it anyway.

It seems that my mother continued to work for the BNA taking on different nursing roles in the West Country, including Bideford and Bath. The West Country was a place that she loved and had discovered on a holiday soon after leaving school. In 1960, my mother was nursing in Bath, she had a flat and that is where she met Kathleen, who was to become a trusted companion for the rest of their lives. Kathleen was also a nurse, working for the same agency. My mother had a spare room and Kathleen needed somewhere to stay where she could sleep in the day as she was working nights. My mother was working days and so this suited them both very well.

At some stage during the 1960's, my father arrived at the flat to see my mother. This was a brilliant piece of the story for me as it means they had in fact been close and had kept in touch. This was following his marriage in 1958 and prior to him working and living in South Africa. I am surprised that my father turned up at the flat, given he had been married to Isabella for two years already, I can only assume that he came to say goodbye. As to whether they had any further contact after that date we will never know. Given the postal service that I have experienced to South Africa, it seems unlikely.

In 1967 my mother moved to Exeter to take on her Assistant Matron's role, soon to become Matron at the Nuffield nursing home. This was her last role before retirement and her marriage to Frank in 1973. Sadly, her husband passed away just before their second wedding anniversary. My mother had been engaged to a gentleman named Gordon after my father. She never had any more children. Such sadness.

| Margaret (mother) as a student nurse 1953 | Margaret as Matron at Nuffield Nursing Home Exeter 1967-70 | First cousin Edna (left) Margaret (right) at Edna's family home in Stockport |

Edna said that she knew she would receive a letter one day about me. She had been watching 'Long Lost Family' and just knew we would meet one day. I asked if she knew whether my mother watched the programme, she did not know and just reiterated that once the decision about the adoption had been made, it was not discussed again. I imagine it was all too painful.

So many emotions have been running through my whole being these last few weeks. I feel like I have taken a ride on an emotional rollercoaster towards the end of an incredible journey, and yet day-to-day, the journey continues. I am getting to know Edna, my mother's 1st cousin, we chat and email quite regularly and in a couple of weeks we will meet face-to-face for the first time. I have emailed a couple of photographs to her as requested, and yes, particularly in one, she could see a resemblance to my mother. Strange how important it is to know that you bear some resemblance to your parents and amazing how strong genetics are; that having never met a parent you can display similar characteristics. My auntie Bet always said I was so like my father in characteristics as well as some physical resemblance, now it seems I shall find out whether I have similar characteristics to my mother as well.

Social media is an amazing tool and I have had people come forward who knew my mother, as a friend, an employer, church warden and simply as an acquaintance. All these snippets of information and stories I am given add to my picture of my mother. It seems that she was a kind and considerate person.

The Sunday after I had received the package, letter and the photographs from Edna, John, and I set off to Exeter, Elaine met us at the railway station in Exeter, unfortunately Philip was unable to come with us. We set off to the crematorium, so that I could say 'goodbye', despite never having remembered the 'hello' to my mother. We passed the entrance and had to turn around, and then we came across a small garden centre and went and found a lovely basket of plants, cyclamens, stocks, a small conifer tree and some other green plants, it really was very pretty. I had of course spoken to the people at the crematorium and found out where my mother's ashes were scattered, also asking permission to take some plants and lay them in the right place. We found the place easily and laid the basket in what I assumed was the correct place. It was a strange feeling, there was no marker to show where my mother and her husband's ashes were scattered. On the Monday I phoned the crematorium again and the young man kindly went down and checked that we had put the basket in the correct place, we had.

After our visit to the crematorium, we went off for a drive to see if we could find the property where my mother and her husband had lived together, their time had been so short. Having driven in a couple of circles, despite directions and sat nav we eventually found the property, we had driven passed twice already. The lady who now lives there was kind enough to show me around, pointing out how the house had been when my mother had lived there. It was a farmhouse, with slate floors, a good solid staircase and lots of original features, all things that I have enjoyed in my own properties over the years. This felt good. Whilst the present owner of the house showed me around Elaine and John went across the road to the local pub, I joined them a little later.

As we drove back towards Exeter, we drove past the house where my mother had lived, after her husband had died. My mother ended her days in a nursing home in Exminster, she had dementia. I wonder whether during her last weeks she ever told the staff about her child, that she had had to part with all those years ago. We went to visit the church that she attended regularly, St Thomas'. We then went and had a meal in town, we were all ready for that, it had been an emotional journey and I was pleased to have had company. We dropped Elaine back to the station and John and I headed home, it is only an hour and a half from Exeter to home.

I emailed Edna, and told her about our day, and following that, we planned to visit her on our next trip up north, only a couple of weeks away, so not too long to wait. Had we not already made plans to go up north, I would have driven up that weekend. As it was with email, letters, and phone calls I had been in touch with Edna several times in the interim, allowing us to get to know each other a little.

At the beginning of October, Ian, my husband, and I drove up to Maidenhead for a couple of days to enjoy and celebrate Ian's older son's wedding. Only five weeks before we had been to Maidstone to celebrate his younger son's wedding. Having had an enjoyable couple of days we headed on up to Merseyside to visit my father's family. This had all been planned some time ago, though now I had some new information to share, which the family were pleased to hear and enjoyed seeing the photographs of my mother. Over the years our visiting plan have changed as the older generation of my father's siblings have died. Our visits were and are always fun, can be hectic, though this one was quite relaxed.

From Merseyside we headed home on a different route than usual. We drove across to Stockport, an easy drive of about an hour. We found our way to the house where my mother has spent many happy times with Edna, where her aunt and uncle had lived and where her 1st cousin, Edna still lives. This was the address that I have had in my possession for over twenty years and that I had been told was a previous work address for my mother. I have a feeling we will be visiting Stockport more frequently from now on.

When Edna opened the door, I felt like I had known her for years, she was welcoming, smiling, and genuine. Ian took himself off to the pub where we were to meet him for lunch. The two of us went into the house and on the table, there were a selection of photographs that Edna had found for me to look at, there had even been some surprises for her, as when she took a photograph out of its frame, containing a picture of my great-grandparents, out fell several photographs of my mother as a child. So, over the next couple of hours I was told a potted history of the family and introduced to family members through their photographs. Of course, I asked a few questions as well, and as usual, I should have made more notes, I had taken my notebook with me. The difficulty with note taking is that it interrupts the flow of information and conversation, making it feel more like an interview. I did say to Edna that I will have so many more questions for her over the coming weeks and months.

When we realised how long we had been talking, we put everything tidy, Edna was kind enough to give me photographs to take away, though I will send them back as soon as I have made copies. Just as we were about to leave the house Edna said that she wanted me to see something that was a part of my mother and we went upstairs. There was a beautiful seascape, framed in a traditional wooden frame. The story is that the painting was in an art shop, or gallery for some time and every time my mother went passed, she

stopped to look at it. When it came to her birthday, her nursing friends clubbed together and bought her the print and then her father, my grandfather had it framed for her. Edna had looked after it for her for years, as when my mother was going to take it to hang in her new home, with Frank, Edna said how she would miss it, and so my mother left it for her. Edna wanted me to have it as it is the only bit of history that she had to give me. I was very touched and felt very privileged that she wanted me to have it. A real treasure, with a history of my mother's likes, as well as her thoughtfulness.

We took the car around to the pub and Ian was relieved to see us, I think he thought we had forgotten all about him, and lunch. We chatted a lot over lunch, I want to know everything there is to know about my mother.

After lunch we returned to Edna's house, had a brief chat, collected my notebook, with very few notes, and said our goodbyes after Ian had taken a couple of photographs. We had stayed for a good part of the day and I have a feeling that we left Edna feeling quite tired. What a lovely day. It has taken so many years to get here and now my journey is at an end, though of course the questions, conversations, and visits both up and down the country will continue.

On our way home, we had an appointment in Exeter to meet a lady who had worked for my mother. After her husband had died my mother eventually sold the farmhouse and bought two small shops, one in Whipton and one in Cowick Street, both in Exeter. Margaret, the lady we were to visit used to work for her in the Whipton shop and had a couple of photos that she wanted me to have. We stayed with Margaret (so many Margarets) for just over an hour and she told me things about my mother, as an employer. How kind she was, how she would always help and care for people. She had two dogs at this stage, a Golden Retriever and a black Labrador which on occasions Margaret would take for a walk up through the fields. It was to this lady's daughter that my mother had lent her set of genuine pearls as her 'something borrowed' for her wedding day and consequently lent the family her car so that they could get to Luton airport to begin their honeymoon. It was clear to me that Margaret had a great deal of respect for my mother and was extremely fond of her.

Naturally, I have so many questions to ask about my mother. Though it is difficult to make a list, as questions are frequently answered during a conversation. Edna had already told me that my mother had visited the West Country and stayed at the 'Old Poppe Inn' at Chard, it is still there, and I feel like I would like to visit sometime. It was on a holiday there that my mother fell in love with the West Country and presumably that influenced where she later worked, and indeed where I was born.

Despite what my adoption records stated, it seems that my mother never went to South Africa to continue her nursing career, and as far as Edna knows, this was never discussed. The only possibility is that given my father was going to work there, it is possible that there was a brief discussion about joining him there, we will never know. Perhaps that is why he visited her in Bath, to see if he could change her mind, though as I said he was married at that stage! Most of my mother's work seemed to have been in the West Country though no evidence of coming down to Cornwall for work. It seems Devon was a favourite place for her. I wonder if my mother knew that my adoptive family lived in Devon.

Sunday 21st October, my husband Ian, and I set off for Exeter to join the congregation at St Thomas' church. The church that my mother used to attend regularly. We arrived just in time for the start of the service, though at one stage I thought we would be late, stuck behind a tractor and a farmer trying to get his fields prepared for Winter. There was a good size congregation and we enjoyed the service. As we left the church we were asked if we lived in Exeter, we explained the reason for our visit, which was to meet some acquaintances and friends of my mother. The chaplain had known my mother well and seemed genuinely pleased to meet us, though he was quite shocked that my mother had a daughter. We walked around to the church hall and joined some of the other parishioners for a cup of tea and a chat. Within seconds, Ian had found a lady who had known my mother through the fund-raising committee. My mother had been instrumental in helping to raise funds for the building of the hall, where we were now standing; with ideas such as buy a brick and 'meat' bingo amongst other 'bingo' ideas. In all we met five people who had it seemed known my mother well. My mother's close friend Kathleen (they had nursed together for many years) also featured in many of the conversations.

My mother was described as a lady who knew her own mind, was organised, assertive and bossy! As my daughter and my sister said, that sounded rather familiar, and from my mum I guess I had the nurture blast of these characteristics. Several people saw a likeness in me, to my mother and one lady in particular said she had quite a shock when she first saw me. People were pleased to share their memories with both Ian and me, it seemed that Kathleen and my mother quite often entertained, raised funds for the church, guide dogs for the blind and the hospice to name a few of their charities. They attended craft groups and made things to sell, they cooked, and my mother was known for her 'tea-breads', I wonder if that is the recipe that I have cooked many times, inherited from my mum and her family in Lancashire. I must ask Edna. I gather that one of my mother's favoured dishes for dinner parties was Coronation chicken, according to one of the ladies that I spoke to.

The Church Warden had known my mother very well and we had quite a long conversation about her work for the church and my mother as a person. Despite being a great organiser and a little bossy, it seemed that both she and Kathleen were popular members of the congregation and gave a great deal of time to fund-raising ideas and events. They are both missed. Kathleen died just a year after my mother.

Following this meeting with welcoming and friendly people we went on our way. We were to visit a lady who had worked for my mother's husband in the office and also her own husband had been the local photographer and had kindly looked out a photograph for me of my mother opening the skittles alley. We went to the village and parked in the pub car park, where Elaine and John had waited for me on our last visit. We had lunch at the pub which was very good and finished just in time for our two o'clock visit.

Once again, we received a warm welcome from the couple who had known my mother. This time, the relationship was different, given that the lady worked for my mother's husband Frank and had done so, I believe, for many years prior to my mother becoming his wife. The husband knew my mother, though not as well, and he had a particularly good photograph of her for me, which I was very grateful to receive as it is one of few where she shows a genuine smile.

The lady and I chatted, and Ian and her husband chatted about various things including cameras and photography. The conversation followed similar lines in respect of my mother and what she was like, the husband felt that my mother was 'posh' though his wife said that she was clever, well educated, spoke nicely, and I added, perhaps reserved. I have been called 'posh' and I think that came from the fact that I did not have an accent, as children we had received elocution lessons at school and our parents did not have specific accents, except when dad was talking to farmers and locals, and then his accent came through. Perhaps the fact that my mother did not have an accent, people had considered her 'posh'. It was clear though that she was well respected, that she was kind to their children and had been approachable in different circumstances, including the sale of a piece of land adjoining our host's shed so that they could keep chickens. We spent a pleasant hour chatting and again I felt that I had added to the information I was gathering; about my mother's life with Frank, her love of dogs and her as a person. I gather she did not join in very much with village affairs, though to be fair, they were married for just under two years and then she lost her soulmate and of course she would have been grieving. She had only retired from her nursing career twelve months prior to Frank's death, perhaps she retired in order to care for him. Following Frank's death Kathleen came and joined my mother at the house, in the interim Kathleen had been working away and would visit during holidays. Together they supported various fund-raising events. My mother bought two small shops, Kathleen retired from nursing and ran the shop in Cowick Street, my mother running the one in Whipton. They must have been terribly busy. My mother was it seemed, the more reserved and Kathleen the extrovert. Perhaps my mother preferred to keep her private life private. She had plenty to keep her busy and continued her fund-raising for guide dogs at Whitstone.

Our final visit of the day was to a lady who was blind and

had known both my mother and Kathleen through their fund-raising events for the guide dogs. She also knew them on a personal basis, enjoying meals and informal get-togethers with them. It seemed that they used to bring their dogs on visits, Silk, my mother's Golden retriever, a gift from Frank, and Haggis a Scottish terrier belonging to Kathleen. This lady remembered her partner helping them to load their dogs into the back of the old Volvo, which I have also heard caused havoc in Cowick Street when they needed to collect or unload stock for the shop and caused a great dealing of horns to blare. They used to walk the dogs on Holden Hill, somewhere that I have also visited, amazing how we have trodden in each other's footsteps on several occasions.

Straight away this lady said how I was tall like my mother, how fond of her she had been and what a good friend my mother had been to her, she also showed me the teddy that my mother had given her eldest son when he was born, called Haggis after Kathleen's dog. Perhaps my mother wondered if indeed, she may have been a grandmother at this stage as well. The grandson was not going to give it up to be looked at, and fair enough, I had a brief glimpse. As we talked there were a few occasions when this lady became quite tearful and I said, careful or you will set me off to. She said that she was so happy that I had visited as now she knew there was a little bit of my mother still there, she had missed her so much; she also said how I sounded like my mother. Blind people have heightened senses to touch and sound and I was surprised, and very pleased that she thought I sounded like my mother.

I felt that I could talk to this lady, she was so friendly, genuine and had a lovely sense of humour, and she cared so much for my mother. I said that I was concerned that anyone may think less of my mother, now that they knew she had, had a child. Her answer was that my mother would feel no shame for any decision she had made, though she would have felt pain. This statement chimed with my thoughts about my mother. She would have thought carefully and made the decision that she felt was the right decision, she sacrificed a great deal for me. I know she would have felt tremendous pain, a pain that cannot be taken away. I am pleased to hear that she would have felt no shame, as there was none to feel.

Everyone that we met that day, seemed to want to share their knowledge, and happily. There was respect for my mother, along with the understanding that she was a strong lady, in charge, assertive, kind, caring and perhaps 'bossy'. The 'posh' bit I think may have been a misinterpretation for being a private and reserved individual, who spoke well. I am proud to say that it seems I take after my mother in at least some of those respects and strive to be caring and considerate. I have been called 'posh', and I will admit to being 'bossy', of course, that is another word for being an organiser and making things happen!

I am so thankful to the people who had been happy to share their memories that day, as without them I would not have come to know my mother in her different relationships.

I still have more to learn and I am hoping that Edna will help me with that, I shall stay in touch with some of the people we have met and hope to visit a few of them again. I cannot tell you how important it is to me to have made these connections. I am aware that no-one is perfect, and I am pleased that my mother was not perfect, as if she were, I would never have been able to live up to her expectations.

People ask me if I had a good adoption, and when I answer yes, they are perhaps a little puzzled as to why I am so keen to find out about my natural parents. I think it is very hard for people to understand that there is still a void, a need to know where you came from, where your roots are, where your name originated from. Believe me it is so important and absolutely no reflection on the family who brought you up. My family will always be my family and now my history and a much bigger family is also a part of me.

Chapter 8

Remembrance Day 100 Years On

Today, between varnishing beams and doors, I found time to watch some of the First World War1 Remembrance. The Cenotaph.

I have always given time to reflect on the war and the aftermath for families and the country as a whole and particularly of course on 11th November. It would be easy to forget that this was a 'world war' and that so many nations and families were involved.

Today I remembered great uncle Thomas Davies who died in WWI just nineteen years of age. He was my mother's uncle, and though she would not have known him, she would have known of him. My thoughts and reflections for today were for all those involved in the WW1 including of course mum and dad's fathers, our Bam Bam's, mum's cousin, Tom's father, my grandfather and his uncles. And specifically, from this year on, for great uncle Thomas Davies, who I have only just found out about, who died in battle 1918.

As Tom, my father was born in 1918 of course that lead me to thinking about him as well. He came home from Dunkirk and was a survivor of WW2.

For me like so many people, my history is very important, and more information can be found these days. Thomas Davies of course was Edna's uncle and she has a lovely

photograph of him in his uniform, presumably taken when he signed up. She has since passed this and other family photos to me, for which I am extremely grateful.

In the final episode of 'The World at War' which I have watched recently, a former soldier was saying that he now feels incredibly rude that he did not speak to anyone in his home village for a year after his return. Having seen the things

Great Uncle Thomas Davies. London Rifle Brigade, died March 28th aged 19. Arras Memorial

that he had seen, he just could not communicate with the others. He found that these people he had known all his life were concerned only with local issues, like what the council proposed to do with the gentleman's lavatory, which to him were matters trivial beyond belief.

It must have been so hard to return to so called normality

having experienced war, and to return as a 'survivor' when so many of your comrades did not. Losing a son, brother, uncle, father, cousin, husband or friend must have been so hard, and for those who were not able to bury their loved ones and to say a proper goodbye, whilst common at the time, must still have taken its toll on the individuals concerned. Few families were spared grief and loss.

Family knowledge is so important, it is our history and our children's history. These days it is so much easier to find out more about people who were in the forces and I must say that I found it very interesting delving into Tom's army history. The only thing I remember linking to the war from Bam Bam on mum's side was that he used to sing 'it's a long way to Tipperary, it's a long way to go ......', it was first sung in music halls in 1912 and first recorded in 1914, so was on the tip of people's tongues to be sung as soldiers were marching along to war.

Chapter 9

Journey to South Africa

My research into the South Africa side of Tom's life is still underway, still hitting brick walls; though very occasionally, getting a glimmer of light, like the fact that thanks to Isabella, I can now visit where he and his wife lived in Observatory. That is the spark that says, carry on.

February 2nd, 2018, I was visiting my son Philip and his family at the farm. Elaine, and her son Freddie were also there. Philip sent a message up from the yard with Daniel to say he would be in soon. He did not usually send messages, if he was about, I would always stop to have a chat and if he was still working, I would not interrupt him and we would catch up next time, unless of course I saw him in the yard. We were sat around the farm-house kitchen table having a cup of tea when Philip came in. Elaine said 'right, can I tell her then?' 'Yes' says Philip. Despite the light-hearted atmosphere I felt a little worry creep in, was something wrong?

Together Elaine and Philip told me that they along with John (who was away on holiday at the time) were going to buy me a ticket to go to visit South Africa. It would enable me to do further research and perhaps find out where my father Tom had lived, and where his remains are; check out where he had worked and perhaps the places he used to frequent. I would also experience the country that he loved so much.

I am rarely speechless, today was however one of those occasions. Tears welled, though I did not cry. I could not believe it, such an amazing gift, why. Apparently because I do so much for all of them, well of course, I am their mother and the grandmother to their children, and I love every minute of it. I hugged them all, Philip's wife Lucy and Elaine's husband Dave and the grandchildren were all part of the planning and this amazing secret they had kept for weeks. I was still finding it hard to speak. What an opportunity. As soon as I got home, I sent a message to my youngest son John to say thank you so much. My children had discussed this with Ian, my husband and I said he had done well to keep the secret, he said he was not sure how definite it was, and he had been sworn to secrecy.

I could not wait, the planning began. Ian had already said that he would be unable to come as he had other commitments and that he would stay and look after dogs, chickens, and the garden. I knew I could not do this alone. I contacted Rosy, an old college friend and asked how she would feel about coming with me on this great adventure. An email pinged straight back to my inbox. 'Yes please, how exciting'. Ever since that day I have been researching the trip, researching more about Tom, and reading about South Africa. Kensington, Johannesburg in the province of Gauteng where Tom had lived, and he worked in Alberton, that much I had surmised from the family and from uncle Dan's letters home. I had rather given up with my research due to constant brick walls, but the excitement of this trip had fuelled my enthusiasm once again. I went through all my notes, contacts, and emails. Had I missed vital information. The one piece of information that seemed to be the key to finding out about my father's life was his South African Identification Number.

Social media is an amazing tool when you need help across the world. I found two sites, South African genealogy and Lost family and friends South Africa, and prior to these two I had received help from UK Aussie Angels. Through the latter, site researchers found the month of my father's death, the date that he and his second wife were married during one of their visits back home to the UK, and, his wife's sister and her South African husband's name, as well as an address in the UK. I knew that Tom's wife, had returned to the UK sometime after he had died, though possibly, ten years later. Now having met Isabella I have their address. I already knew that Tom had a niece, his sister-in-law's adopted child, born in South Africa I have been told. Some of this information has come in triplicate, uncovered by the other two groups. A real stroke of luck and clever investigation by these researchers has led to finding Tom's Identification Number. I was so ecstatic with this new information; it should move things forward. The generosity of these people who research on behalf of others is endless, I cannot thank them enough. No question too small and no search too big. I have been astounded at what they have uncovered for me, like the ID number, which I have been trying to access through official channels for nearly twenty years! So perhaps now I will be able to get the access to Tom's estate, which will then lead me to work records and endless information that I would like to have in my possession.

Eighteen months ago, I had put in another official request for details about Tom's life in SA. At that stage I still did not have his date of death or his ID number and so I have heard nothing at all. I am told that this lack of response is not unusual. At the beginning of April 2018, I sent another email, this time giving the death details for my father Tom and his ID number. I also asked for a response so that I knew the information had been received, which they kindly did for me. The information was sent to the Master's Justice Office Pretoria. I have about nine months before my visit to South Africa and I am hopeful that I may now receive the information I require.

I re-read through uncle Dan's letters, those written to

uncle Derek and to auntie Betty. All the letters had the same address of his lodgings and so I sent off a letter to that address. Appreciating that it was twenty-eight years since the last letter was written. Uncle Dan always referred to his landlords as being a 'young couple', that suggests that they were younger than him and therefore possible that they could still reside at the same property. Uncle Dan was clearly fond of the couple and had lodged with them for some time. Sadly, no response received. There were some other towns mentioned in uncle Dan's letters, Midrand, where he lived, Germiston, Cyrildene, Braamfontein, Durban though no other clues. These seem to be places where uncle Dan socialised or where he worked, having described himself as a hobo, he travelled to where the work was available.

I put a message on the South African Genealogy group to ask if anyone could recommend a guide or a local historian who might show me the older parts of Kensington, as it was in the 60s to 70s when Tom lived there. I had a gentleman come back offering to help me with my search in Johannesburg area and he could recommend a guide for us. Again, such generosity. I must be honest that I did google the gentleman as I have heard so many horror stories about safety issues in Johannesburg. I found him on LinkedIn, and he was exactly what he said he was. I like to be trusting and I struggle currently with having to be so cautious. This gentleman, Raymond has said he would like to help me get closure, along with knowledge and adventure and knew that I would love the country.

Each time I meet up with Tom's family I get another tiny piece of information that may help, and recently Aggie sent me a business card that she had found in auntie Betty's belongings, it had Tom's writing on the back with a telephone number and my contact in SA, (Raymond) thinks this may be useful.

So, by mid-June I have booked us a three-day safari at Kwa Maritane Lodge. Well, you really cannot go to South Africa and not do that and a safari has always been on my 'bucket list'! I have booked accommodation near Kensington, in Houghton, so that we can continue research into where Tom lived. I am looking at the Premiere Class train to get us down to Cape Town, it seems that is the safest, unless you can afford the luxury of the Blue Train. I think we may then fly back to Kruger to continue our adventure, maybe visiting the Drakensburg Mountains. I have also looked at how we can visit Blyde River Canyon, Pilgrims rest, Long Tom Pass and the Bourke Potholes all recommended by a friend of Ian's who lived in SA for many years. Things are coming together. Oh, and I have finally booked the flights, getting a good deal with Qatar airlines.

I have written to six crematoriums as Auntie Betty told me that Tom had been cremated, to ask if they have any information for me, and as usual no response, despite having included my email address. I wrote to some hospitals in the Kensington area as my father must have been a patient at some stage, considering his army record and regular admissions, also the fact that he died of cancer. I have written to uncle Jim's sons to see if they have any details about where their father used to stay with Tom. I have recently heard back from cousin James and he is going to have a look through some boxes he has in the loft to see what he can find for me. I have written to the main library in Durban, as suggested by one of the social media sites to ask about old telephone directories as that may be a way to confirm Tom's address as the photograph shown to Sue and me by Isabella may not have been their most recent address. To date I have no new information, perhaps the postal service in South Africa is as bad as people say it is! With every stamp goes a glimmer of hope and excitement so I keep going.

Raymond has kindly agreed to pick Rosy and me up from the airport and if I hire a car he will then act as our guide in Johannesburg and for the Blyde River part of our adventure. I have bought DVDs about South Africa, both from a political perspective and from the holiday, touring aspect and these are proving very useful in determining our itinerary. Rosy and I are meeting next week to discuss the plans and then Raymond is going to have a look and help us edit if required. After so many emails, I feel like I know this man already. I did get a little carried away with the planning and almost missed our opportunity to take the train through the Karoo to Cape Town as I had forgotten that the train only runs on a Thursday and I was hoping to visit the coastal area where the logger-head turtles' nest and lay their eggs. South Africa is such a huge country, so much to see, so much diversity, I can see already why Tom was hooked. For two women travelling alone there are constant warnings about safety issues and taking this into consideration does make the arrangements slightly more difficult. I am so grateful to Raymond for all his help and advice and that he is going to do some local research about Tom, which may save us some time visiting libraries and crematoriums.

It is so easy and yet pointless to do the 'if only', though I still ask myself why I put things off for so long. I suppose the fact that Tom had already died when I met the family, I learned everything from them, and yet so many things I still need, want to know. Not having found my mother before her death, I have been unable to ask her for memories of Tom. I would urge anyone, in a similar position to me, to ask the questions, follow the leads and to remember that sadly when we lose people, we lose the information that they carry with them. For me, and perhaps for you, I did not know what I needed to know. I did not know how important it was for me to know. Now that I know, those memories are lost, taken to the grave by family who knew. I am so lucky that I still have a few cousins who had met Tom and who occasionally remember a story or find a photograph and think of me. I am so grateful for that. On my mother's side, thank goodness for Edna.

In the DVDs that I had ordered I was interested to see a

small clip about the power generated. Half of Africa's electricity is generated by South Africa. There is a network of pylons that deliver electricity to three million homes, schools, hospitals and factories. Sixteen thousand miles of cable carrying four hundred volts of electricity across the country. Tom was a part of providing and installing telegraph cables back in the days when he worked for BICC, travelling through Africa for his work. Telephone cables frequently line up alongside the electric cables and pylons on their wooden poles as we have in this country. That is quite a legacy. That particular DVD was released about eleven years ago, so a little after Tom's death, though he would have been involved in the process of this amazing provision for Africa. These days engineers are airlifted onto the pylons to undertake repairs, which is a risky business; it is wonderful how civilisation moves on and yet it is important not to lose the beauty of the land, or to take away the traditions of the people.

My research continues and some changes to our itinerary have been made, so that we do not waste time and money, going back on ourselves. We have some amazing places to stay and wonderful places to visit. Following my recent contact with Tom's wife, I now know where they lived together and am still researching, with the help of others to find where his remains lie, so that I can go and say goodbye as well as the hello, that I never had the chance to say. Land registry has shown that Tom and Isabella lived in that same house for all their time in South Africa until after Tom's death when the property was sold for the first time since it had been built.

December 2018

For what seems like weeks now I have been having regular visits to the Doctor's surgery for concoctions of vaccinations, polio, diphtheria and tetanus, hepatises A, measles, mumps and rubella (mmr) x2 and rabies x3 and of course malaria tablets at the ready. It was time that I had some boosters as it is probably thirty years since I had a tetanus and that was because I had injected myself with sheep wormer! The sheep jumped as I was administering the injection and it went into my hand; the doctor seemed quite amused at the time and said, 'not to worry at least you won't get worms!'

Finally, I have managed to book the three internal flights and after numerous emails I have booked and paid for the transfer to and from the safari at Pilansberg. We will be collected from our address at Johannesburg and then returned to our address at Pretoria, at least that is the plan.

The excitement along with the apprehension are growing steadily. Naturally, I am thinking, have I organised everything, will it work out, have I considered the risks and taken the appropriate precautions as advised, and in relation to my research. I have ensured that I have ample medication for my heart condition, 50 and 30 factor sun cream, insect repellent, vitamin B1 to prevent being bitten in the first place. So next on the list is clothing, taking as little as possible. Clothes that will be suitable for city, safari, beach, train, walking and of course flying. Oh yes, and flight socks.

We have a weight limit of 20kg for all flights and there was also a recommendation for size of luggage for the train, I cannot find it now, though I think we will be fine. Long sleeve tops and light trousers are a must to keep the mosquitos at bay in the evenings. Plenty of space will be required for souvenir gifts for the family, as without them, this trip would never have happened.

Boxing Day. A quiet day I thought. Finished the itinerary, checked the tickets. Thank goodness, I thought. I had already gone through everything, checking and double checking. Though I had indeed made a mistake with the British Airways flight from Cape Town to Durban. I had put my name as Cathy, the name that I am always known by. The ticket of course must be in the same name as my passport, Catherine, the name my mother had given me. I made the call immediately and the lady on the end of the telephone was brilliant. Firstly, she asked other departments how to go about the change, unfortunately my executive club account, where my Tesco points add up, is in Cathy, not Catherine and so it could not be changed without changing that as well – which for some reason was not as simple as it sounded. The lady eventually said that she would stick her neck out, she said 'it is obvious to us all that Cathy is short for Catherine' The call lasted over half an hour and the exorbitant cost was £1.50 for my ticket to be changed! I cannot tell you how grateful I was to that young lady. If she had not changed it, we could have had real problems at the airport and Rosy and I may have ended up on different flights, leaving us even more vulnerable as solo female travellers.

At the last minute I had a message from Raymond that he was very poorly and would not be available to help us at all. He had been bitten by a tick and had encephalitis, he had been hospitalised and was very sick. Another lady who I have met through the genealogy social media page has now offered to collect us from the airport as she said that will be one of the places where we would be most vulnerable.

So now, we are, fully organised and ready to go with our full itinerary.

South Africa Itinerary

Fly Heathrow 8th January 20.30pm arrive Doha 06.15, depart Doha 08.40, arrive Johannesburg 16.35 9th Jan

Arrive 9th January Johannesburg Airport 16.35pm Brenda Collecting from airport. Stay at Houghton to 15th 6 nights Booking confirmed Airbnb

10th chill, shop and check out plans for week? Use pool etc

11th? Visit Jewish Quarter and drive by or visit 35 Klip Street.

12th visit Apartheid Museum

13th? Gold Reef City /? rest day

14th markets / Botanical Gardens (15th Pilansberg until 18th Safari) Kwa Maritane Lodge +27 14 552 5100 3 nights

BOOKING CONFIRMED Booking.com transport out and back with Tautona Tours and Safaris

18th to 20th Pretoria Heatherdale Guesthouse 2 nights BOOKED. Meet up with Brenda

20th to 22nd Mountain Sanctuary Park Magaliesberg Mountains BOOKED. Transport will be Uber x. Magaliesberg Mountains

23rd return to Johanessburg Reef Hotel Booking.com 1 night, transport Uber x

24th Johannesburg to Cape Town train Africa Sun Travel 1 night BOOKED AND PAID FOR Premier Classe Train Shosholoza Meyl Railways booking.com Johannesburg Railway station 9.30 by Uber x

25th Cape Town 4 nights Booked Possible pick up from station, need to confirm, if not Uber x

Table Mountain and walk down through Kirstenbosch Gardens

Robben Island

? Signal Point (sunset)

Boulders Beach penguins

29th Fly Cape Town to Durban BA6309 13.20 ARRIVE 15.20

29th to 31st Dolphin Coast 2 nights Airbnb

Confirm pick up from airport or Uber x or hire car

31st to 1st Feb Shakaland Beehive room 1 night BOOKED Zulu Cultural Village Normanhust Farm, Eshowe. Transport back to and from Durban Airport hire car or Uber x

Flight Durban to KRUGER KJLADH depart 13.45, arrive 14.45 Hire a car

Feb 1st-5th Daans at Graskop 27 Monument Street, 1270 Graskop. (4 nights) Booking.com Raymond's contact to show us around?

Blyde River Canyon, God's Window, Bourke's Luck potholes, Long Tom Pass

Pilgrims Rest

Drakensberg Mountains

5th Flight Kruger to Johannesburg KEWOOF depart 13.35, arrive 14.25 meet up with Brenda, tea and cakes, return phone!

Feb 5th Flight out from Johannesburg 20.35, Doha 06.15 Depart Doha 07.55 return to GATWICK 12.25 6th Feb

It all looks, so simple doesn't it. Watch this space!

Sunday 6th January 2019

Two days and we are off. Still so much to do. I have packed, and re-packed, a couple of times now. I think I have sorted everything out and packed within the weight limit. I have decided the easiest way is to take older clothes and things that are now a little too big for me, they will be cooler and then instead of bringing them home to go to the charity shop I can leave them behind for someone who may be able to make use of them.

My affairs at home are organised and Ian, my husband will be able to sort out any blips along with Clare who is looking after part of the business. Today Elaine and Freddie have been up for the day and to say their goodbyes to me. Tomorrow I am taking Bethany out for the day, she is not happy about me being away for four weeks. Monday I will spend time with Dan and Matt after school and say goodbye to Philip, Lucy, and John then of course Tuesday morning to my husband and my dog. We will be driving up to Heathrow, Rosy's partner is driving, and then kindly collecting us from Gatwick on our return.

The adventure begins and our journey's journal is written

Tuesday 8th/9th January 2019

We left home at 9.15am once Ian had managed to find his car keys! Met Rosy and her partner at Bodmin and after a quick goodbye to Ian we went on our way. It will be a long time to be away from home, the family, and Bertie my dog.

We stopped briefly at Exeter services and again just after Bridgewater at a great farm shop, (note to self, visit again). Another quick stop about half an hour from Heathrow and then on our final run. Having had our bags wrapped and checked in I realised that I had left my flight socks in the car and so had to purchase another pair, doctors' orders. We were advised to have our bags wrapped by Brenda my friend in South Africa, for wherever we flew in South Africa and certainly from Heathrow. Most people, including South Africans seemed to have the same idea. From my perspective, my case is quite old and at least the wrapping would prevent all my personal belongings spreading out over the carousel. That would have been an embarrassing start to our travelling. Due to my heart problems, it had also been suggested, by the airline that we had 'special assistance', so we went to find out what we had to do and also it gave me a chance to wrestle with my flight socks! We walked through to the security where I had to wave my pacemaker card to say that I could not walk through the security booth. After being searched, and finding Rosy again, we were taken to the special assistance lounge in a buggy. We had a two and a half hour wait before boarding which gave us time to read and for me to put the first notes in my journal.

We had a great view of the airport, though neither of us noticed how few planes were taking off or landing. I was getting pretty excited at this point, up until now it seemed as if this whole trip was a fantasy, something for me to plan and keep my mind busy over the last year but would never actually happen, excitement mixed with anxiety. In the waiting area was a TV and we noticed that it said something about no planes able to land or take off at Heathrow due to drone activity. Again, it did not sink in until other passengers started talking about it. Lucy rang me on my mobile and asked what was happening and, in the background, Philip said, send Rosy to go and sort them out, it will be quicker than waiting for the SAS! Someone went off to ask the staff what was going on, apparently the staff knew nothing about it. Our only concern was that we might miss the connection from Doha, though at this point there was nothing we could do about it. We had a delay of one and a quarter hours once we had boarded, and then, off we went up into the night sky leaving London lights twinkling beneath us as we headed towards our great adventure.

We left at 21.45 eventually and had a good flight to Doha apart from our rather noisy friends behind us who were constantly pulling on our seats as they kept moving about, never mind the snoring and other interesting sounds. It did not dampen our enthusiasm, though made it difficult to sleep. The food and the attention from the stewardesses were good, we watched films, read books and slept, though not much. We made up time and landed at 3.45am our time, awaiting the last leg of our journey. We only had about forty minutes before taking off again, just long enough to freshen up and stretch our legs. As we flew over Khark Island into

Doha the sun was rising over the sea, beautiful colours, yellows, and oranges stretching out towards us, welcoming us.

We flew up the Gulf of Oman towards Aden, Gulf of Somali Basin and were four hours from our destination, Johannesburg. Even then it did not feel that we are actually going to spend the next four weeks in South Africa. Perhaps I had done the trip too many times, on paper, over the last year already.

We experienced a great deal of turbulence for about half hour of our flight and were confined to seats with our seat belts on. During our flight I noticed that we were flying at an altitude of 10972 metres at a speed of 560mph and -47 degrees outside. I am aware that these figures will have changed during the flight, and I thought that the grandchildren may have been interested, especially Dan. Rosy managed to jam her seat belt and it took a little while to free it from the side of her seat. The seat belt sign remained on. We only had an hour and a half left before landing and the anxiety was rising. We have been warned so much about the risks in Johannesburg and to be fair most airports worldwide are not the safest places to spend your time. My eyes keep filling with tears as we approach the country that Tom loved so much and being aware that he would have landed and left from this same airport on so many occasions, only the name had changed. I cannot really believe that I have come this far, in miles or emotions, from the Quill Box all those years ago, it held so many secrets. However, the only reason that I am finally visiting the country that my father loved so much, is thanks to my children, their spouses and my grandchildren, though the latter were not too pleased about me being away for so long, and all were the root of my emotions. During the final hour and a half flying into Johannesburg, I could not believe I was going to finally land in Tom's home city.

An exhausting couple of days, both physically and emotionally and so, so worth it to arrive at the start of our journey. Brenda, (who I have been chatting to through one of the South Africa social media sites) and her husband John met us at the airport, it was such a relief to be collected and driven to our Airbnb, where we stayed for the next six nights. Our accommodation completely exceeded our expectations, a great start. Brenda and John stayed and had a cup of tea with us. Brenda kindly lent us a South African mobile phone with data already loaded and ready to use. They both gave us some sound advice about staying safe. I got the impression that Brenda was quite concerned about our plans. We will be meeting again before we leave, perhaps when we are staying in Pretoria as that is where they live, if not then, at the airport for a meal before we head home. Brenda was amazing, helping to find out about Tom and is still grappling with Home Affairs over his death notice, on my behalf.

Since meeting my stepmother, and confirming where my father and she lived, by pure coincidence we are staying just seventeen minutes' walk from their house, though of course being Johannesburg, it is not safe to just wander over there by foot.

Tomorrow we will do some exploring of the area, once we have worked out how to use uber, to hail a taxi. We will buy some fresh salad, vegetables and fruit to nourish us whilst we are here. It will be sad that we cannot just have an amble around the neighbourhood, but that is something we will just have to adjust to for the time being. Strange not to be able to take a walk in the park, there are so many trees here. Luckily, our garden is sizable, and we will be able to sit outside and wander there. Tomorrow is the first day of our African Adventure.

10th January

I had a great sleep after taking painkillers for my arthritic hip and my poor bruised legs, still hanging on since a nasty fall over a tractor bucket New Year's Eve at home. And no, no alcohol was involved! My room was large and airy. I woke at 6.50 to songs of garden birds and spotted a pair of brown birds similar to female blackbirds, though larger with slightly long yellow beaks, they had a good song to sing. Turned out they were myna birds.

It is unlike me to be wake so early, probably the excitement, anxiety and confused sleep pattern from the journey; as well as anticipation of what lies ahead. No sound from Rosy's room so I guessed she was still sleeping and so I listened to the bird song whilst I sipped my fennel tea and contemplated. There was a good breeze and the willow tree was swaying in rhythm, the agapanthus gently nodded their enormous blue heads in time with their surroundings. The garden was lovely, the sky was a little grey though there was already some heat in the sun. I could hear traffic, people off to start their day, I wondered if a siesta was common practice, and therefore started their working day early. We are close to the main road, though it was a fairly quiet night – I did not hear anything anyway.

I looked at google maps and realised how incredibly close we were to where Tom had lived. I wondered if his mornings began as mine had, with the same sounds and scenes. There was a roll of thunder, light rain fell and lightening flashed, despite the grey sky, it was warm. That may be a regular occurrence due to the altitude and the fact that there has been a heat wave for a few weeks. I read that thunder and lightning storms are quite common around Johannesburg in the summer months. The light rain soon cleared, the lightning abated, the sky turned blue and the day was beautiful.

Never mind the weather anyway, today is for relaxing, doing a food shop, checking out the location and perhaps a drive-by to Tom's house and Observatory itself. The weather does not and will not interfere with our plans. And when it was dry, we had a great garden where we could sit and acclimatise.

Today was about planning our next few days and checking our itinerary. Rosy had found that a family of campers were attacked the night before New Year's Eve at the Mountain Sanctuary where we will be staying next week. The man was hit over the head with a large stone. There were children in the tent, thankfully not hurt. My view was that whilst that must have been very traumatic for the family, the security would be improved following the event, making our visit safer and no need to cancel, we have booked to stay for two nights. I would however keep this information from the family for the time being, until after our visit. We will not be camping; we have a cabin booked which can be locked and secured.

We managed to organise the uber having set up the account which took some time! We went to Norwood, suggested by our host as being the closest place to shop for food unless we wanted to go to the mall, which we did not. We had lunch at a café, again recommended by our host we had shawarma (wraps) with falafel, quite delicious. Then had a short walk up the street, the only white people on the street, ending up in a café across the road from the shop. We were ushered to the back corner of an empty café where we had rooibos tea. We felt that having two white people in the café was an embarrassment and would perhaps stop black people coming in. It was clear that we were not invited to sit outside on the street to have our drink, though no animosity was shown towards us by the staff, it felt very strange, perhaps the boot was on the other foot and we should have considered the community more carefully. We drank our tea, paid, and left. We did our food shop and awaited our uber return fare. We were conned, the driver said he had arrived, and we were not there so I was charged twice. When he did turn up, I asked if he had already been to collect us and he said 'no!' Whilst annoying, this was not going to spoil our day. We had shopped where Tom may have shopped and enjoyed a local area and managed uber, quite an achievement.

We had wonderful fresh fruit, salad and vegetables, nothing force-ripened, all beautiful and ready to eat. We returned to Agartis Cottage before 5pm, not knowing at what time it might get dark and told that we must be back before dark. We then had to get our way through all the security, the main gate, the garden gate, the front door and then put the alarm system on. All very different from what we are used to. We had not visited Tom's house today as we have to work out exactly how uber works, it does not seem easy to add a destination once the initial booking has been made, perhaps tomorrow morning before we visit the Apartheid museum.

Just before five o'clock I went out in the garden to watch the weaver birds who were making quite a noise and darting around collecting food for their young. As I came indoors the sky was darkening, smothering the soft blue of the day and the temperature was dropping. By five fifteen an amazing thunder and lightning storm began, starting with light rain drops, and progressing very fast to giant plops of water falling from the sky, then came the lightning, giant ragged cracks of sharp led light against the grey sky. The thunder rolled and bellowed overhead accompanied by the lightning and cracks like a whip snapping in the air. By five thirty-five the thunder seemed to be rolling away and the lightning had run out of power. And then the thunder returned, it felt as if it was delivering blows directly to the roof above my head. By five fifty the storm had passed, the rain cleared, and the sky looked lighter. That was a big storm with great velocity that lasted far longer than those I am used to at home.

11th January

The garden at Agartis cottage is beautiful, encouraging an abundance of bird life, weaver birds, myna birds, luminescent cape glossy starlings, ibis flying overhead and many other cheerful birds, that are heard, though not seen. It is stocked with masses of agapanthus, huge blue heads enjoying the sun and nodding in the breeze. I had not realised that these are a native flower as we have an abundance of them in Cornwall and in the Isles of Scilly. A massive, ancient willow tree dominates the lower part of the garden and beside it is the tree hosting the weaver nests, woven carefully onto their host tree. There are several nests of different ages and yet several seem to be in use and parents are feeding their young, they are very noisy birds and chatter to each other loudly. They dart around, you just see a flash of bright yellow as they dive and dash all over the place. Many birds land in the garden on their journey, though they do not stay long enough to identify them, it is a shame that they move too fast for the camera to capture their beautiful plumage.

Today the sun was scorching, and I took my breakfast outside, to soak up the rays. I only stayed out for about ten minutes and then went back indoors to write up some of my thoughts and to put some sun cream on. We organised an uber to take us out to Tom's house on Klip Street, before the telephone battery died for a second time. The driver, Thabani, was helpful and waited for us whilst we looked around and took some photos of what would have been Tom's garden. We met the house boy who had come to collect the bins and I asked if it was ok to take some photos, explaining that my father had lived there many years ago, he said it was fine, so long as I took a photo of him, which of course I did. He said that Tom was before his time, though he had remembered the previous owner well. With the security fences and gate, it was difficult to see very much, and we were not sure that we had actually looked at the right house, though we were at least clear about the garden! On the way back we stopped so that I could take some photographs of what had clearly been, a beautiful park, now a golf course, I wondered if Tom and Isabella had walked there sometimes. I was sure that Tom would have walked when he could and enjoyed the open space, so green, beautiful, and lush.

The house is set high above the road and must have had wonderful views across the hills and valley, even better than the views today. The gardens are amazing and the whole place is so private and green. It was a short visit that meant a great deal to me, to have walked in my father's footsteps, just a few steps.

I left a note with the house boy Zondi, for the owners explaining why I would like to visit. I do hope that they respond.

Things became somewhat frustrating when I tried to get hold of uber to take us to the Apartheid museum. The battery having been on charge for hours simply gave up. I downloaded uber to my own phone and started the process all over again and had all the same problems that I had with Brenda's phone. When I next need an uber I will nail it!

We booked a tour for tomorrow to visit Soweto (So)uth (We)st (To)wnships and the Aparthied museum which will be interesting. I have heard a lot about Soweto when it was still Sophia Town, from my uncle Dan who also lived in South Africa for about fifteen years. He wrote several letters to uncle Derek and auntie Bet.

Today however was not wasted, we researched what we wanted to do for the next few days, we have our itinerary, and just want to make sure that we have made the right choices. I had a walk around the garden as I was feeling like I needed exercise, it is strange to be confined all the time, albeit for our own safety. I decided to walk a dressage course as it seemed silly just walking around in circles, so I tried to remember one of the ones I had done about fifty years ago. I felt better for it, despite not having a horse to ride, I had a purpose for my walk!

We sat in the garden and watched the birds and I even managed to get a couple of photos, though not of the cape glossy starling with their bright red eyes. I finished reading my book, one less in my bag for travelling home. I also found that some of my mosquito spray had leaked in my suitcase and so I had to rinse things out and wipe out my case. At least I will not get a swarm in my case.

12th January

An interesting and an eye-opening day today. We were collected from our accommodation at 9.30am and met up with the rest of the group outside of the Apartheid museum. Firstly, I had to explain to the security lady that she could not use the security swipers on me because of my pacemaker, once she understood, she searched my bag instead. Having got through security we were given random tickets by our guide. My ticket said BLANKES WHITES, Rosy's ticket said NIE-BLANKES NON-WHITES. This meant that we had to use different entrances to access the museum, mine was an easy gate followed by a passageway with posters to read on the way and then a ramp to walk up to where we all met. Rosy's group took slightly longer to come around as they seemed to go through a longer passageway and then had to walk up a flight of steps this was to signify the constant struggle for the black people on a day-to-day basis. The final slope that we walked up had mirror images of people who had strived for success in South Africa, both black and white. Some of those people made it to the top, others did not. Once we entered the museum, we found out more about their personal struggles.

The museum was fascinating and very intense. It took you through the Boer wars and the South African war. It explained the 'Long Trek' taken by the early Dutch settlers when they realised that they could not fund another war against the British. After two and a half hours we felt the overload. The news reel from the Apartheid time, the stories and photographs, were a lot to take in and for me the most poignant room was the one where there were nooses hanging from the whole ceiling representing those who were hanged during the Apartheid atrocities and alongside each wall the names of each individual, and the date that they died.

This made me wonder how Tom had coped, and what his thoughts were about Apartheid – given that he had already witnessed the Anti-Semitism towards the Jews during the second World War. I know that Tom worked with Afrikaners and learnt the language as he felt he needed to be able to communicate directly with his workers. I believe he picked up some of the local languages as well, though back then black South African's individual languages were not respected and they were expected to speak English or Afrikaans. The whole time that Tom lived in South Africa there were uprisings, reprisals, death, and destruction, and yet he loved this country, always.

As we left the museum, we could clearly see The Seven Pillars of the Constitution, Democracy, Equality,

Reconciliation, Diversity, Responsibility, Respect and Freedom. This constitution was drawn up between 1994 and 1996 by South Africa's first fully democratic parliament. The museum itself had been completed in 2001 and was about South Africa coming to terms with the past and working towards a future that South Africa could call its own.

Following our visit to the museum we were driven to Soweto (South West Townships), we were shown the upper-class, professionals' homes. They were mostly secured by electronic gates, some also had razor-wire, and a few had electric fencing, we were however told that it was a safe area for people to live. My uncle Dan mentioned Soweto in his letters and talked about the 'posh houses' with all the security. At the time he was in South Africa, Soweto had taken the place of Sophia Town, he said.

We continued to our lunch venue, which was in the Soweto Towers, both of which are graffitied with advertising, these change quite often according to which company has commissioned them for advertising. The towers also double as a night club, despite being open all day. We were treated to some Africa dance and then our Brai (BBQ) arrived at the table. There was no choice given, there was chicken, goat, sausage, pat, coleslaw and a spicy sauce. Not quite what we had expected, but ample, though I have to say I had a chicken wing and stuck to the other non-meat products. It was not particularly good food, considering it formed part of our day tour package, perhaps it was designed to teach us a valuable lesson about having food on the table and sharing it with the flies. It all added to the ambiance.

On our way from the towers to Soweto Township we were taken to see the huge football stadium, it is built in the shape of a calabash, an Africa pot, and designed to seat around 80,000 people. Surrounding it we saw the gold mine slacks which are all around the city and were apparently about to be re-mined as it has been shown that a great deal of gold slipped through the original mining process and there is still plenty to be re mined from these slacks above ground. Somehow the wealth of the gold and the money spent on the stadium highlights even more the poverty of some, or most of the people living here.

We moved on to see more of Soweto, the difference between rich and poor was horrifying. The middle-class homes, small, though tiled roofs, brick built and adequate were on one side of a narrow road and on the other were shacks. There are properties allocated to families, though the waiting list, we were told could be fifteen years and if you found work in that time, you were no longer entitled to a house. This did not seem a good way to encourage aspiration in people. There have been situations where a family had been allocated a house, then an official comes along evicts the family and sells the property to someone else, so not much security in your own home, even when you have had one allocated. The sheds which used to be single occupancy for the gold mine workers are used for housing, though I have a feeling this is more like squatting. Electric is bypassed and a mass of wires are hung together like spaghetti on the poles to provide electric to the sheds. There is a port-a-loo standing in the middle and the driver told us that this is an area convenience for any number of people, not an individual one for a family. They are supposed to be emptied every other day, though frequently it could be three-weekly.

We stopped to have a half-hour conducted tour around part of a Township. We were shown around by a young man who was smiling, happy, proud to be showing us what happens in his home environment. It was clearly one of the poorer communities and yet the people were friendly, smiling, proud and keen to show us their homes. We were shown a shack that had been painted to celebrate Youth Day 16th June, this was the creche for the younger children. Further down the lane we were invited to go up into the school room, a rickety, tree house type construction that looked out over the tops of the shacks around it. This was the school room for the older children. A young boy and his baby brother were watching their teacher perform a mime for us to see. What sticks in my mind were the broad smiles that we received from everyone who lived there and the excitement from the children. Possessions are fairly non-existent, a few chairs could be seen under the trees mostly for the older generation, the youngsters happily sat on the ground, or playing games together, older children taking care of the younger children. Every washing line was full of brightly coloured clothing and the children were immaculate, despite the sewage running down the lane. One of the little boys, probably about six years old noticed my personal alarm, I had forgotten it was still attached to my rucksack. He was fascinated by it and I had to try to explain that there would be a terrible noise if he pulled it, he was laughing and smiling as he ran along beside me still watching the alarm.

From there we went to the site of Nelson Mandela's house and drove passed Desmond Tutu's house as well. Mandela's house is almost empty as the Apartheid museum is adding another exhibition with some of the furnishings from the house. I was not sure why this area was referred to as the 'real' Soweto, where we had just been was indeed, very real. I believe that it was simply that Nelson Mandela chose to live in the area alongside some of the most poverty-stricken families. There were a great many street traders there and as Rosy and I were not looking for souvenirs at this stage given we still had a long way to travel on our adventure, we opted out and stayed on the mini bus watching people moving around and bartering for their goods. I was feeling emotionally and physically exhausted at this stage, it had been a very sobering day. I had left a donation for the school room hoping that the school would benefit, so did not have any cash on me for souvenirs now.

As we drove around Johannesburg, we saw mothers and their children sorting through rubbish that had been fly tipped along the roadside. The children were barefoot and there was a great deal of broken glass from bottles mixed in with the rubbish. The refuse collection was very haphazard and so the people collect as much recycling rubbish from the tips and then they can sell it to the recycling depot for a few rand. It is not just mothers and children, it was just that today, it seemed to be more often women than the men collecting the recycling, though we often saw men pulling great dumpy bags of recycling along the road, or pushing it on a cart. The goats were also mooching around to see what they could find to eat.

Our final stop of the day was the Hector Peterson museum, it was the square of Orlando West that we were visiting rather than the actual museum. Our guide told us of the events. In his own words, it was here, that on 16th June 1979 fifteen thousand children/students came together to protest against the introduction of Afrikaans and English as a medium for instruction – these children did not speak or understand either language. Following a scuffle concerning two deaths of administrative staff, the burning of dogs, police and education buildings, the police used tear-gas and then opened fire. Six hundred school children/students died that day, thousands were injured and the youngest to die was Hector Peterson, just thirteen years of age. The date of 16th June was named as a national youth day by Nelson Mandela and is now a national holiday for the youth of South Africa.

Today was fascinating, sobering, upsetting and helped me to learn far more about what Apartheid actually meant, and how important education is to the young people of this country. I brought two bracelets for my granddaughter, the money going towards caring for people with HIV and Aids, the colours and patterns signifying the struggle that South Africa has endured for many years.

There was a small tribute to Tom during this day of learning and reflection; we saw the Telkom tower and a great deal of overhead telephone cables.

Having spent several hours reflecting on our day we started to think about Tom's house. The only way I could think to find out more was to post a picture of the house and ask if anyone recognised it, Isabella had let me take a picture of her photograph. I put a post on South African genealogy as the people have been so helpful over the last year, including Brenda. I received a lot of advice about finding deeds of ownership initially and then suddenly a post popped up from a lady saying, my goodness, that is my neighbour's house! I messaged her straight back and will await a response.

13th January

A lovely day after the most galactic thunderstorm yet. Funny to think that I am seeing and hearing the same things that Tom heard, the amazing thunder and lightning in the evenings, the torrential rain and then waking up to the bird song at 4.00am now.

Today having got Brenda's phone working again, we arranged an uber for 11.30 and set off to the Botanical gardens. There are security guards at each of the three entrances and the advice is, if you visit during the week, make sure that you are with a group of people; if you visit at the weekend it is much safer due to the number of people and families that frequent the gardens. It was the weekend.

This was the first day since we arrived in Johannesburg that we felt free to walk outside, enjoy the sun, enjoy the area and to feel safe. I hasten to add that we have not felt unsafe at all, though we are constantly being told to be careful and 'stay safe' – it was bliss, the freedom to amble that we take so much for granted when at home. The temperature was thirty degrees or more, we made the most of the shade offered by the enormous and ancient trees that formed avenues in parts and coppice in other areas. We wore our sunhats and plenty of factor 30.

We explored Shakespeare's Garden the Rose Garden, and the Huguenot's Memorial Garden. It was peaceful, despite the amount of people also enjoying space and the sun, meeting up with friends and family, many seemed to be celebrating birthdays and other celebrations were going on, shopping trolleys loaded with packages from cars were wheeled over to their picnic spots by the porters and people were selling balloons, it is obviously a popular venue for family events. Some people had tables and chairs, tablecloths even.

We walked down to the Emmarentia Dam and found a nice sheltered spot to sit and eat out own picnic. We had

Southern Masked Weaver birds to join us, chattering away to each other, feeding their young who seemed perilously close to the water. The nests had been woven onto trees that reached out over the water, perhaps this was good to keep the young safe from predators, though I wondered how many were lost in the process of venturing out and learning to fly. We were also surrounded by Egyptian Geese, or South African Geese, indigenous to South Africa.

After our picnic we explored more of the gardens and found an area that was separated, fenced with a seat, and tranquil. We saw a South African Hoopoe bird which was really quite striking, having only seen one in books before. We also saw a Hadada Ibis, initially Rosy thought it was a pigeon, I was describing it as large, grey with some iridescent colouring, a long back and tail feathers, at which point it turned and I saw the long-curved beak. Definitely not a pigeon. We had both been focusing on different birds, looking from different angles!

So today we have been to Randburg to visit the gardens. The Botanical Gardens developed from the original Rose Garden, established in 1964. The Botanical Gardens now cover 125 hectares and are looked after by the city council. The opposite side of the dam offers hire of kayaks, small sailing dinghies and paddleboards, people were certainly enjoying their day in this inviting, well-kept environment.

We thoroughly enjoyed our day and felt relaxed and safe at the park. I had to go to the café and ask the young man for help with the phone, as it once again decided not to switch on. With a quick removal and return of the sim card we were back online and able to order our uber to take us home. We had done a lot of walking today and were feeling quite tired, affected by the heat as well I suppose.

I felt sure that Tom and Isabella would have enjoyed the gardens and perhaps kept an eye on the developing of them from the original Rose Gardens. From the photographs that I have seen of both of them, I think that fresh air, exercise and open spaces may have been high on the agenda for relaxation time.

I have had a message from Jane, in response to me putting the picture of Tom's house on the social media page in respect of visiting Tom's home. Jane has given me the contact numbers for her neighbours and for her husband, she says that we can see a lot of Tom's house from their own property. We are running out of time as tomorrow we leave Johannesburg. However as Rosy said this was one of the most important things I wanted to do whilst I was here, so somehow, we will make it happen. I messaged the people who now live at the house.

14th January

Our last day in Johanessburg. We set off to visit the elephant sanctuary near Hartbeespoort Dam. Uber worked and our driver duly arrived, with no idea where he was going to be taking us. He was young, and new to uber, poor fellow had to ask me for a sub so that he could get fuel for the journey. The sanctuary was about an hour and three-quarters journey! I gave him R100 and off we went, getting fuel on the way.

We had an interesting drive, new scenery, always something to see, though I would have been quite happy not to have seen the sign 'Hijacking Hotspot', we are however still here to tell the tale! When we arrived at the dam, we realised that we were going to be about five minutes late for our tour and so rang the sanctuary and explained. When we arrived, we went straight in and joined the group, we were not the last to arrive. After about five minutes one couple dropped out as there was quite a lot of walking on uneven gravelly ground which was quite slippery, there were one or two slips for people, added to which it was very hot at about 34 degrees. I love the heat, so not a problem for me.

We began by walking through the monkey area and were warned that one particular monkey was prone to pick-pocket, he had his eye on us and we kept a good eye on him! There was quite a walk to go in order to meet Amarula, he was an elephant about to be culled and was saved by the sanctuary, he had a habit of sitting on visitor's cars at the game park where he had lived previously. He clearly did not like the noise and fumes invading his space. He was damaging cars extensively and had to be culled or moved. Amarula, yes, the same name as the liqueur which is made from the Marula fruit. People are often selling this fruit on the side of the road, or the middle of the road, particularly at traffic lights and junctions.

Amarula is a huge, fifty-year-old male elephant and he was waiting on the hill with his handler. It was quite a walk and involved walking close to an elephant stopping electric fence at 5Kv, this unnerved me somewhat as I have to be particularly careful around electric fences amongst other things due to my pacemaker. If it can knock out an elephant of his size, it would certainly set sparks flying for me! However, I was careful, breathed in and moved around the fence very cautiously. When we reached the elephant, we each gave him double handfuls of nuts, feed, not peanuts. He had a whole bucketful and as his handler said this is just a light snack for him. The nuts were put into his up-turned trunk, he then blew the feed into his mouth, he was quite happy to be patted and fussed, there were no restrictions for him and yet he stood happily eating his treats.

Having all had a turn feeding Amarula we traipsed down to the seating area, where we were to be told a little more about the habits and anatomy of elephants, for example an elephant's heart weighs 7kgs. Due to the pads on their feet which act as shock-absorbers, you do not hear them coming unless they snap a twig or scuff the gravel. They are very quiet creatures, in movement anyway. Two female elephants duly arrived, unheard. They stood in the enclosure with their handlers. We were able to scratch behind their ears, see inside their mouths with their huge molars. Elephants go through between four and six sets of teeth during their life, partly because they use their jaw back to front rather than side to side which wears out their teeth.

As a parting shot the elephants gave us all a kiss, or rather a suck on the chin. Their trunk is turned upwards, and they suck on your chin for their kiss, rather a messy procedure I have to say, that leaves you covered in wet red soil and snot. Thankfully there is water to clean yourself off and Rosy had wet wipes with her! One gentleman was given a kiss on his rather bald head, he looked as though his feet were going to lift off the ground. It is a very strange sensation.

The final interactive opportunity was to walk with the elephants, this meant walking in front of them, with your hand gently holding the upper part of their trunk, as in the opening. They would offer their trunk to do this and then happily walk behind. It was rather lovely despite the initial thought of the sheer size of this animal immediately behind you.

Whilst all of these activities were very much part of the elephant's regular day, it was quite clear that they were happy, the handlers were gentle, quiet and clearly cared for their animals. The young man showing us around had started working at the sanctuary when he was fourteen and was now twenty-eight, still enjoying, and genuinely interested in the welfare of these beautiful animals. There was an easy relationship between the elephants and the handlers, no raised voices, no sticks, no reprimands, just genuine, mutual trust and care for their charges.

At the end of our two-hour session, we were escorted back through the monkey area. Rosy and I sat in some comfortable chairs and helped ourselves to a cup of tea. We were chatting to each other and did not realise that everyone else had disappeared. We found ourselves locked into the area where on occasions people stay so that they can be involved for a full day and night with the elephants. We eventually found someone to let us out and made our way into the shop. Clearly everyone else had somewhere to be, even the shop was empty. I bought some rulers with wildlife depicted for the grandsons and then did my best to book an uber home. Initially it looked as though I had been successful, though having walked down to the main gate and stood in the extreme afternoon sun for forty-five minutes, we realised I had not.

To get a signal I had to return to the shop. I tried again and it said no uber available. We had a cold drink and sat under the mango trees before trying again. Apart from mango trees, there were banana and avocado trees, with notices stressing that all the fruit is grown for the animals. Lucky animals I say.

We gave up with uber as we were clearly out of their range, the girl in the shop kindly rang a taxi for us and said it would be about an hour and a half as Lawrence, the driver was in Pretoria. So, off we went for a look around and found the meerkats, not my favourite animals, though I have to say that they looked rather sweet stretched out under the tree trying to cool down with their bellies on the earth.

After a while Lawrence arrived and seemed very surprise that we knew immediately who he was. He was telling us that he used to be an uber driver, he had been attacked twice by his passengers and decided to set up his own company, doing more chauffeured driving, as well as airport transfers. He had a couple of drivers working for him and had bought nearly new cars, BMW seemed to be his preference despite the very comfortable Toyota that we were travelling in. Lawrence stopped at the dam for us to look and to get some photographs and then took a couple of photos of us with my camera. On the approach to Johannesburg, we saw a herd of goats in the central reservation, sleeping and eating, with no-one looking after them. It is a wonder none of them were knocked over on their way there, or perhaps when they decide to move on again.

As we neared Johannesburg the late afternoon skies became darker, the heavens opened, the thunder rolled, and the lightning struck. This was far worse than we had experienced before, the rain turned to enormous hail stones and the torrents of water became rivers across, and beside the roads bringing rocks, gravel and other debris with it. Trees were falling across the road, either from lightning or from being pulled up by the floods. It was dangerous driving; cars were stopping in the middle of the road as they could not see what was happening. People were running, trying to get away from the huge hail stones, grabbing their belongings as they fled. We were pleased that we personally were not driving in this weather and Lawrence did not seem fazed by it at all. As we approached Agartis cottage the rain stopped, though the thunder and lightning continued. The garden was covered in white hail stones.

We had enjoyed a busy day with up close and personal contact with elephants and learned something about them and the care that they require. They were happy elephants, last seen playing in the water pool as we left.

A plate of fresh salad and fruit was a good end to the day and an early night, as we were leaving the next day.

15th January

Up early to be packed, cleaned up and ready to go by 10.00am. Our driver Jeffrey who is taking us to our safari destination at Pilansberg, arrived early, and I managed to set off the alarm by mistake in my panic to make sure that the driver did not take off without us. Lusungo, the caretaker of Joao's property where we had stayed, said it was not a problem, the security guards would have realised it was a false alarm.

I felt sad leaving Johannesburg as I felt I still had unfinished business, though I felt quite confident that I may still get to see Tom's house in a few days and perhaps find out a little more about how he lived his life here. There have been some developments on the South Africa Genealogy site that have given me hope.

Jeffrey, not his given name I imagined, African people are given English names when they go to school, talk about ripping away their identity and heritage. Jeffrey was however a talkative, well-educated young man and a good driver. He works at the Kwa Maritane lodge as well as doing transfer driving. It seems that his family farmed, as he talked about going home and having cows, though one had died during the draught. We had a two-and-a-half-hour journey to Pilansberg and so it was good to have a driver who was interested in the surroundings and was happy to share his knowledge. It is great to see the scenery and even better when you begin to understand what structures the colour and shape of the land before you. We had already found out about the gold mining and slack hills around Johannesburg, and the plan to re-mine those slacks with more refined machinery as it appears there is still plenty of gold in those hills. There are also zinc and lead mines along with the coal and perhaps best-known, the diamond resources. A land so rich in minerals, with silver, fluorspar, and quartz which all have uses in the industrial world.

I noticed a small herd of Shetland ponies grazing alongside zebras, which was a bit surreal. As we drove, Jeffrey pointed out open-caste platinum mining and further along the road, smelting platinum and underground mining with an underground air system, we saw more as we came close to Pilansberg. We learned a great deal about the mineral wealth of this area from Jeffrey as well as all about the different crops and farming. Jeffrey also told us, for my son Philip's information that most of the dairy farms were in the Bloemfontein area part of the Free State, where there were larger farms where fencing was cost effect in keeping the herds together in better pastures to provide quality milk. South Africa has Jersey and Guernsey herds along with Holstein, Ayrshire and the Brown Swiss which originates from European Alpine areas, as the name suggests. Most of the cattle we had seen so far were beef cattle which roamed along roadsides and on rough ground and were then moved to the homestead at night for safe keeping. The next day they would be walked along the verges to take what they could get before once again returning home.

When we arrived at the Kwa Maritane Safari lodge, we received a warm welcome and were offered cold drinks and shown to our room. Two queen size beds, a culturally decorated room, and a view from the balcony with trees, an abundance of birds, both large and small including a go-away bird and the masked weaver, the latter we had come to know quite well.

We were quick to book our first game drive as we did not want to waste any time; we had a couple of hours to explore first. We checked out the pool, shop and the hide, which you go through a long underground tunnel to access. On our first visit we saw a toad, lizards and some interesting birds.

The first game drive was wonderful, our driver Hendrick

was not actually a ranger, he was just helping out today. His main job was to apprehend poachers in the park, and he was deeply knowledgeable about a lot of the animals, including his main concern, the rhinos. Pilansberg is a National Park area.

Within minutes we saw an elephant, a young male, he was not interested in coming close though he did progress parallel to us for some time. We saw kudus and lions, again too busy to take notice of us. The first rhino we saw, a white rhino, came out of the bush and crossed the road right in front of the truck, he was chasing a female with her calf. Hendrick told us that whilst the mother could protect the calf all was well, but if the male wanted to mate, he would kill the calf to get to its mother. We saw blue wildebeests and one had two calves running along-side, we also spotted zebras, the ones with brown, black and white stripes, the common zebra, not the black and white which are the cape zebras. We saw several birds, though at this stage we were unable to identify them and as the evening drew in, the bird song went quiet. To complete our list, we saw warthogs and a mongoose strutting its stuff with its tail high in the air. On our drive back we spotted a chameleon sitting in a bush, the lights from the truck showed it up, a luminous green.

Our drive was supposed to have been three hours, however Hendrick stayed for four hours and showed us everything possible that was now prowling around having rested in the midday sun. The bush was alive and our trip exhilarating. We did stop for a snack and a drink; it was still very warm, and it was dusty driving around the tracks. The environment is quite amazing, both land and sky seem to be unending. Thankfully there had been some rain and the vegetation was green and lush, providing good food for all the inhabitants. Pilansberg is an area of 55,000 hectares, 20 of which are not accessible to the public, though all of it is open to the wildlife.

The issue of poaching was very real, and Hendrick's job a difficult one, he, his team and dogs do not have the appropriate resources, like night vision binoculars, good quality radios etc. He told us of a situation where he and his team had apprehended a gang of five poachers and their van, in which they found a large amount of cash, found in a box concealed under the vehicle, the dogs sniffed it out, R90,000,000, equivalent to over £5,000.00. Within the fifteen minutes it took to arrive at the police station the lawyer was already there and yet as far as Hendrick was aware no one had had a phone to call him as they had been confiscated. A few days later the poachers 'escaped,' and the cash deposited with the police had disappeared.

Poaching continues and will do so for two main reasons, money and greed. The market is still there even though scientists have proved that the rhino horn contains no more than keratin, which we have in our own hair and nails. The market is in Asia and Vietnam because people still believe that the dust from the ground horn has healing powers. Whilst those beliefs continue, so will the poaching, because the rhino horn is worth the same as gold on the black market. Whilst there is corruption there will be poaching. Hendrick has a thankless task. Where there is demand, money, and corruption; poaching will continue despite the horn having no healing powers at all. The only way to stop poaching is through education, dispelling the myth that the horn has any healing value.

This evening we had our tea outside under a lightning sky, stunning, and not one drop of rain. There was a huge choice of food, so delicious and so difficult to make a choice with the spread available. It has been 38-40 degrees all day today and so a cool evening was much appreciated.

My head was buzzing with what we have seen. I don't know what I expected to see, but the vastness of the bush, the wild animals and the randomness of what we have seen has just been totally mind blowing, words cannot really describe my thoughts.

16th January

I set my alarm as we had a very early start, I rarely get up before sunrise these days! Today though the game drive was to leave at 5.30am and we had to be at the truck by 5.15am, actually we were in plenty of time and had time for a cup of tea and a rusk, before we left. The day was already warm, though we had put on an extra layer for the early start.

Jola was our ranger and driver for this morning. We

entered the park at a different gate and the scenery was different from yesterday, we seemed to be in the bowl of the volcanic crater, with the mountains rising all around us.

We saw a young male lion before we even entered the park, he was facing the rising sun as it rose over his kingdom. He made no move when he must have heard the truck approaching just a few meters away. I suppose as these trucks are no threat to the animals, they have got used to ignoring them. Once we had entered the park and had a drive around looking for wildlife, we came across two cheetahs. I felt privileged to have seen them, they are so fast, and I thought generally quite shy. One was sitting up and the other lying down, both enjoying the early morning sun after perhaps a busy night hunting. They seemed unsure whether they were going to rush off or stay and stretch out in the glorious sunshine. One of the cheetahs had a collar on, to keep track of where they travel, I could not see clearly whether they both had.

Shortly after seeing the cheetahs, we came across two other game drive trucks who were waiting patiently in the hope of seeing a leopard. The leopard had apparently made a kill and had dragged it up into the tree, as they do. She had no intention at this point of leaving her kill, and so after about twenty minutes Jola asked if we wanted to wait or move on. The consensus was to move on, most people seemed only interested in 'The Big Five' and wanted to see what they could. I must admit that I was happy with the scenery, the bird life, and whatever animals we happened upon. I was thoroughly enjoying the whole experience, the excitement and the drive, the scenery was exquisite.

There was a rather embarrassing situation though that happened after we left the site of the leopard. There seemed to be a strange noise coming from the truck. Everyone started looking around them, including the driver. Rosy suddenly said I think that is your alarm. I said I did not have an alarm, having completely forgotten about the personal alarm on my bag. I must have dislodged it slightly when moving my feet and set the alarm off. I found it and stopped the noise. When we stopped for our break, I spoke to Jola and apologised. Thankfully, it had not happened when there were animals about. Jola said that with the noises of the trucks and the radios it was not a problem. I did feel rather silly about the whole thing though and the alarm was put in the suitcase as soon as we returned to the lodge and stayed there for the remainder of the trip!

We saw blue wildebeests again, two of them having a great time running and jumping around, we saw more kudu, a water buck, a tsessebe, the fastest of all antelopes. On the bird front we saw the pied kingfisher who really was quite striking, we also saw what looked like rocks in the water, but on closer inspection found them to be a family of hippos. What a delight, I had not even thought about hippos. When we returned to the spot two and a half hours later, they were still there. They come onto land to eat at night, returning to the water to rest during the day. Whilst they looked as though they were floating, they were actually standing on the bottom of the lake.

Whilst having breakfast and looking over the pond, we spotted a crested barbet and several other birds which we were unable to identify at the time.

Just after 3pm we had returned to our room and heard a commotion going on outside, from the balcony we were surprised to see two baboons scratching and eating the bark from the trees and then continued their rampage between the lodges. A female then arrived with a baby on her back, following her was a large male, who then took off in another direction. Rosy went off to the shop to get some postcards and was then heading down to the hide. I stayed and watched from the balcony for a while to see if I could see anything else. As I walked inside, I noticed on the web cam that a pair of rhinos had appeared at the water hole, likely I am told to have been a mother and daughter, as the young males go off on their own to find their mate and establish their own family. I grabbed my camera and quickly made my way down to the hide, hoping that Rosy was already there.

Lucky for me the rhinos were still there, in fact they had laid down in the mud on the edge of the pond to cool themselves. They were rolling and using their tails to spray water over their large, hot bodies. Rosy had been there when they arrived and taken some great photos. The rhinos stayed for about half an hour after I had arrived and then got up and went on their way. We saw several birds at the water hole, including the weaver birds and the blacksmith lapwing and the pin-tailed whydah.

Not long after the rhinos and Rosy had left, I heard what seemed like quite a large, heavy animal coming down the left side of the hide, not usually the approach for the larger animals. It made me jump back when I saw the large male baboon come down within touching distance. It was followed by a smaller one, a female I imagine who looked directly at me, as if to say, I have seen you, I know where you are; she was followed by the whole troop which included three very young baboons. The female that had made it clear she had seen me and could have accessed the hide herself, stationed herself between the hide, me and her young. She then hid herself in the long grass initially, when Rosy returned followed by a father and child the female baboon began to look quite threatening and made it quite clear that we were intruding on her space. We left as the last thing we wanted was a grumpy baboon inside the hide! We had the delight of seeing the troop playing in the tree along with the youngsters before we left. It is surprising how noisy baboons are when they arrive, perhaps it is their way of scaring off other animals, announcing their presence.

This evening we met a new group of people and were driven in the game vehicle into an allocated place in the bush, it was secure and set out beautifully, a place built for the occasion of the lodge Brai (BBQ). There were wonderful salads, vegetables and plenty of meat and garlic bread. The chefs from the lodge had put on a great spread and the meat was all cooked in front of us. There was also an array of fabulous desserts. Being fussy I would have preferred chicken to beef and lamb kebabs, though the selection was good, and salads amazing, so absolutely no cause for complaint.

The whole area was lit up with lanterns and a huge fire pit with a wonderful raging fire. The fencing ensured that no meat-eating animals came to join us on the off chance of an easy meal.

A wonderful day, followed by a very atmospheric evening, stunning location, great ambiance, and plenty of delicious food.

17th January

Woke up early for our second early morning drive. Today our field guide was Eugene and what an incredibly knowledgeable chap he was; he knew about all the creatures in the bush, birds, animals, reptiles and the warning sounds that certain birds make which had helped him to wait sometimes and see animals that he would have missed without those warnings, such as the African Civet. There was some cloud in the sky this morning and though balmy at the lodge, once we got out in the bush there was a pleasant, light breeze. It seemed that this slight change in weather may have made all the difference to the number of animals that we saw this morning.

On our drive into the park, we saw children walking to school at 5.45am and families piling into cars to take their much younger children to school or nursery. I am not sure what time schools open here, though I am pretty sure that few children at home would be happy walking several miles into school, and look happy about it at that time of the morning. African people certainly know how to walk, whether they choose to, or must is almost irrelevant, it seems it is what people do, part of their culture. It certainly keeps people fit and gives the children the right idea, that you must make an effort to achieve your dreams and aspirations.

The first creature we saw today was a puff adder, Eugene spotted it lying in the path of the truck, he got out of the truck and found a long stick. Having made sure that we all saw the snake and told us that whilst they do bite and you would feel very poorly, you would not die. He then carefully moved the snake to a safe place and off we went again. Of course, even the rangers are not supposed to leave the truck, Eugene made sure there was no danger in the immediate vicinity whilst he put the snake in a safe place. We encountered a few herds of blue wildebeests, one with a newly born calf, literally within a couple of minutes, the afterbirth was still with the mother and it was wet and on the ground. Whilst we watched, he staggered up, and within five minutes he was racing off across the bush with his family – in the same way that a new-born domestic calf or any other creature might do. Nature is quite amazing.

We came across herds of the common zebra. No Cape zebra. Zebra and giraffes travel together, protecting each other, we were told that the zebra when it bites, will latch on tightly and the giraffe can kick in all directions and so together they keep their predators at bay.

We saw rhinos, hippos and a pride of eleven lions who were lying quite close to a herd of impala, both watching each other carefully. Mountain antelopes from a distance, up on the rocks and we saw the tracks of a black rhino and hyena which Eugene showed us, though we never saw either. A pair of elephants made an appearance, two lone bulls, they leave the group once they are 'teenagers' and go off to find their own herd. A rare sighting today was of the Pilansberg water buffalo, a group of four who posed for us long enough to take some good photographs. Wart hogs, birds of prey, ox peckers, laughing doves, a pair of steenboks, mountain reed buck and a black shouldered kite were all on our list of amazing viewings today.

This morning was a revelation, amazing viewings in this beautiful park, around every corner there seemed to be something new to see and more herds than we had seen before, we have tended to see just one of two of most animals except for impala. To see these herds of animals in this beautiful environment was far more than I had expected. The large herd of giraffes were beautiful, so graceful with their long necks looking like barley sugar sticks, from a distance. It shows how well the environment supports these animals as several are producing young and surviving well, expanding the herds. There is plenty of space for young males to go and find their own new areas where they will then set up their own herds.

This afternoon we had a rest, staying by the pool, enjoying the cool water in the heat of the day. We also spent some time down at the hide, we were there when three kudus arrived at the water hole. Such majestic creatures with their amazing long spiral black horns and horizontal stripes on their faces, vertical stripes on their body. We saw a number of birds, though some were so fast that we had no time to identify them. The colours that become evident when they fly are so bright compared to how they look when they are still, for example the red winged starling.

This evening we did our fourth and final safari with Jola as our field ranger. The landscape was so changeable, rugged, yet exotic, and the volcanic mountains with the craters are so dramatic and look very different in the evening light. It is so difficult to hold these pictures in your mind when around every corner there is a new view to admire. Photographs whilst working as great reminders, sadly do not capture the essence of the light, the animals, or the landscape.

This evening we were a smaller group and having had such an interesting drive this morning, it was difficult to imagine how this evening would compare. However, we saw rhinos, giraffes, wildebeests, zebras, lions, wart hogs and far more elephants than previous drives, including a very young one, possibly days old with its mother, slightly removed from the rest of the group. We had previously seen a young zebra, wildebeest and rhino.

This evening hippos were on the agenda, along with a giant egret and other birds, including collared doves and laughing doves. We had already heard the spiel and taken a number of photographs and yet each drive has been different, the animals travelled so far in the course of the day, it is unbelievable, and because they have moved to different areas the photos were all different because of the changing scenery.

We had in fact taken the same route as we took this morning, I suppose I was looking for the animals to be in the same place, as they would be in a zoo, but everything looked different, due to the dense vegetation, ample grassland and water. And the animals had travelled quite some distance during the day. This was real 'wild' landscape and animals. It is such a joy to see and so difficult to actually put into words. During the day, apart from the impala the animals seem to have split into much smaller groups, or perhaps they were different groups to the animals we saw this morning. We came across a group of four rhino and I wondered if this included the male who apparently had a habit of charging the trucks, though Jola did not mention it.

The clouds were gathering, and the sky was becoming a darker grey as we got back into the truck after a refreshment break by the Mankwe Dam. Looking across the dam from the hide there, we saw a herd of water buck and impala with a couple of wildebeest – it was so peaceful and the reflections in the water were perfect. We were becoming used to the African skies and the galactic storms and to the strikes of lightning illuminating the skies and mountainous scenery; it had been a regular occurrence every other day since we had arrived in Johannesburg, though so far, we had not had rain here.

Jola seemed in quite a hurry to get back and whilst we did stop to see more giraffes and elephants on the way, we passed a lot of other animals, admittedly animals which we had already seen this evening though still worth watching; he had done this before and so it was not a surprise, he was not someone to give more than the allocated time slots; it was frustrating, perhaps especially as this was our last drive, we leave tomorrow. Jola was not one for giving explanations.

The lightning continued and soon electrified into fork lightning, so dramatic against the dark grey sky, with yellow, red, and silver rays of the sunset. The truck was moving so fast now, despite the ruts, red dust, and stony surface. Dust blowing in our faces and hair, making my hair feel like wire-wool and my face looked as though I had been sunburnt with red dust stuck to the sunscreen I still had on my skin from earlier. The truck swaying violently from side to side. I knew Jola liked to stick to the time allocation, but this was ridiculous.

A storm was coming, fast and furiously through the bush. The wind was now at full force, we had noticed this as a regular occurrence in the evenings in the bush. We were travelling in an open sided truck, with canvas roof, with various splits in it and the driver had even less protection above him.

The rain began steadily, growing in ferocity soaking everyone and everything in sight. Jola suggested that we should unroll the side flaps and whilst we did so he made his own area as waterproof as possible. He pulled the cover over his head and dropped the panel between himself and us where the rain was penetrating and soaking everyone. Rosy and I were pleased that we had sat a few seats back this evening though all the other drives we had sat up front. On we went again, holding down the sides of the truck as the wind was too strong for the velcro, which should have held them in place.

The truck rattled, the storm raged, thunder clapped, and lightning forked, striking the sky like spotlights. Jola drove fast to get us out of the bush as quickly as possible, the rain was running rivers down the tracks; clearly, he wanted to get back onto a good road surface as stones were being dislodged by the water. We were thrown from side to side as the ruts in the road became deeper with the water dislodging more stones and dirt.

We were all handed plastic ponchos, which whilst a good idea in principle was a little late and having two hands holding down the sides meant it was rather a performance trying to get one over your head!

It was thrilling, the elements battering everything, the lightning lighting up the universe only to plunge it into darkness within seconds. Being cocooned in the truck somehow added to the already dramatic atmosphere. Not seeing where you were or where you were headed, surrounded by intermittent light, roaring wind and raging rain was one of the most surreal experiences I have had in my life.

At the back of the truck there was a family with two young boys, possibly eight and ten years of age, they were shrieking and laughing, and I thought, this is an event they will remember all their lives, the truck, roller coaster ride, out of the bush. I wonder if they will also remember the amazing animals they saw.

So, our final game drive was as exciting as all the others, just in a very different way. I could not help thinking where did all the animals go, did they stay together in their herds? Did some get frightened and separate and would this make them very vulnerable when the storm subsided? Or perhaps they were so used to these storms that they just continued with their business, as usual. I was a little sad that we would not witness the aftermath of the storm tomorrow morning.

18th January

Woke at six o'clock this morning to the continued rolls of overhead thunder. The air was fresh, and it was light outside. Rosy was up and off to the hide, I stayed to sort some things out and finish packing. I kept an eye on the web cam so that I could run off down to the hide if something exciting turned up. Later I joined Rosy at the hide, only birds this morning, with so much rain last night the animals did not really need the water hole. Just as Rosy was about to leave and do her packing and have a shower a beautiful woodland kingfisher arrived, with wings of turquoise blue and a bright red beak. I stayed and watched for about an hour. In flight the turquoise was stunning darting across the pool for some very small fish and skaters I suppose, then back to the tree to eat. We both managed to get some good clear photos of it and a short bit of video.

We met up at the restaurant and had a wonderful breakfast, we then headed for the pool and sat writing our journals and relaxing until our lift back to Pretoria arrived. It was good to see Jeffrey again, he was a steady, safe driver and so knowledgeable, a mine of information and happy to share his knowledge about his country including the state of politics in South Africa, sharing what he knew about the area. We talked about open cast mining of chrome, the rich red soil full of iron, he told us a story about marula fruit trees and why the fruit was so small, it is so that heavy fruit does not fall on your head from such a great height, he said God made sure that the people and animals, shading under the tree would be safe. He was genuinely interested to find out what we had seen and done over the last few days. Jeffery's favourite animal is the giraffe and Rosy and I agreed that we loved them, so majestic, they seem to live in slow motion and always two legs moving in rhythm unlike horses who have a variety of movements.

As we drove along, we saw plenty of cattle grazing along the side of the road as usual, and Jeffrey said that is why the meat is so lean, because the cattle can only graze there in the day on the rich grass and are moved at night for safety reasons. There are dairy cattle, though not many farms in this area are big enough to be able to fence the dairy cows in. They need to be cared for more than the beef cattle. He knew of one farm that milked about 250 cows near Johannesburg and thought the farm may be near Braamfontein, he had mentioned this before and I got the impression that he had checked his facts for me.

We arrived at our guesthouse in Pretoria after a two-and-a-half-hour drive, though it did not feel that long. Jeffrey had very kindly escorted me to the pharmacy on our way as I have had very bad hay fever. I never thought to bring tablets with me, despite the fact I had remembered the sun cream! Our host in Johannesburg had kindly given me enough tablets to get through the few days we had been on safari, and now I have run out. I went into the shop by myself and the pharmacist was extremely helpful, unfortunately I did not initially recognise any of the drugs and then she found one that I knew. As I was about to pay, I saw Jeffrey standing beside me and he just asked if I was ok. There were no white people in the area at all and I think he thought I may feel vulnerable. It was exceedingly kind of him, and I was grateful, though I was feeling quite ok and everyone was helpful.

As we arrived at the gates of the guest house, I felt quite relieved as it looked better than it had online, an old colonial building, with lovely gardens. It took some time to get someone to come to the gate, eventually they did, however they then disappeared. Jeffrey helped us to unload our cases and off he went, checking several times that we were happy to be left, he seemed concerned that there did not appear to be anyone meeting and greeting us. Rosy and I went into the house, we were met by a Jack Russell dog who seemed quite welcoming. We walked through the lobby; it was like the Marie-celeste.

'Fawlty Towers' had nothing on this place. We stood in the lobby of this old house, surrounded by lots of furniture and precious possessions housed in glass cabinets for about twenty minutes before someone turned up, even though we could see someone at a sewing machine through a glass partition. We called, nothing. Eventually two girls came in, smiling and friendly, apologising that they had been out the back. They showed us to our room, which had been made up as a double. I asked if it could please be separated into two singles as I had specifically booked a twin room as we are not a couple. This seemed to cause some hilarity for the girls, and it seemed that the owners had thought we were a couple, so still giggling, the girls changed the room around.

Whilst they were doing this, I noticed how many adapters and extension leads there were, to my horror they went off to find another one as the bedside lights would not work otherwise. The system was totally overloaded. We do have a ceiling fan which is a relief as the temperature is 31 degrees in the shade at 5pm.

Having immediately removed as many adapters and plugs as possible, we settle down to read and to watch the beautiful garden birds, such vibrant colours, I don't know why we were surprised, colour is evident everywhere we have been so far in South Africa.

At six thirty, one of the girls, Patience came to tell us that tea was ready. We were the only people eating at that time and were faced with a variety of dishes on a hot plate. We did not know if more people were eating or just us and therefore had no idea how much we should take, or even what the food was. The table was set with full cutlery and so we assumed that dessert would follow the main course which seemed to be some kind of chicken and rice dish, some frozen green beans and frozen mixed veg. It was pleasant enough and thankfully we both eat meat as no choice had been offered and we had not been told what the food would be.

Having finished our main course, we waited. And waited, thinking that Patience would remove the dishes and offer us some dessert. Patience reappeared, to ask what time we would like breakfast and then announced she was off for the day. We soon realised that Patience just about ran the guesthouse and worked twelve to thirteen-hour days! So, we eventually got up, took our dishes to the kitchen where I helped myself to an apple. We returned to the Marie-celeste, and our room to continue reading.

19th January

After a somewhat lumpy start to the night, referring to mattress and pillows, when I sat on my bed both ends of the mattress shot up in the air, I felt like I had been sandwiched. Once I managed to lie prone the mattress seemed to recover itself and went down again. The pillows were very lumpy and looked as if they were stuffed with rolled up old socks and felt like it to. Tiredness eventually overcame us and with the help of the ceiling fan, we managed to get some sleep. The upright fan was too noisy to be left on, windows cannot be left open, particularly on the ground floor because of security and the only other option was to leave the fridge-freezer open, we did for a short time, though obviously not all night. Once prostrate on the bed it was not too bad, though getting to that position was interesting. At least I was not lying there expecting an electrical fire to break out; having removed as many adapters as I could previously. At the time I had not considered that all the other rooms in the house could have been just as overloaded. Rosy's bed seemed better behaved than mine, though I would not have wanted to lie under the ceiling fan, it was somewhat precarious looking. It took a while to work out how to switch it on and when it started and went off at full pelt is looked as if it would fly off and spin about the room like a helicopter. Eventually I worked out the settings and it slowed, appearing slightly more stable.

We had a quiet morning reading, sending WhatsApp messages home and updating journals as well as watching the garden birds. Sat in the sun for a while, but soon moved to a shadier area. The pool was in the middle of what appeared to be a building site and did not look very inviting, so we stayed away from that. Even Bertie, my dog would have turned his nose up at the green soupy looking water! This was supposed to have been a day of rest and relaxation by, and in the pool, I had taken a long time finding a property that had a pool, knowing that this was to be a quiet restful day. Patience asked why we were not swimming and we asked her if she sometimes swam, she said no, she could not swim and would worry that her children may find her face down in the pool, so we let the subject drop.

I had finally received messages from Jane again about Tom's house. After several attempts it seemed clear that the neighbours were not about to invite us in. Perhaps their lack of communication links to the security issues and vulnerability that many white people are feeling at the moment, from what we have been told. Also, it is their home now and I could understand why they might not want to show someone around who they knew nothing about. I had been invited by Jane to contact her husband Tony and to visit their house if we had no luck with Tom's house. So, I booked the uber to go back to the house that we now knew was Tom's.

Lawrence's driver arrived at 2pm and we set off back to

Klip Street in Johannesburg, it was further than I thought. I rang the bell at Tom's house, no response. So, I rang the bell at the neighbour's house and Tony kindly greeted us. I had called him previously and his wife Jane had told him about our likely visit, he was only too keen to help. Tony was Irish and so straight away seemed interested in Tom's life. He told us a lot about the area and what it was like to live there. He and Jane have lived there for almost twenty years, so whilst they never knew Tom, they knew the area well and also knew their previous neighbour, who it seems had bought the property from Isabella after Tom had died. The present owners have only lived there about nine years.

Tony told us what the house and garden had been like when he and Jane first moved to Klip Street. He also explained that given the house was built in about 1960, that Tom must have been the first owner and had perhaps even had it built. He went on to explain that most people quickly planted loads of trees around the property to stop the dust from the goldmine-dumps. As we have seen the wind can certainly get up and the rain lash down. It seems that Tom would have either planted the trees or paid someone to do it for him.

We had a look at the beautiful views from Tony's garden and he said that the layout was very similar to how Tom's was and still is, with its swimming pool on the lower terrace. We were able to take photographs of what had been Tom's home, though we were obviously careful not to be too intrusive. The present owner's car was in the car port, so I think it must have been to do with security issues that she did not want visitors, and given the area, the electric fencing, security gates and armed response teams, I do not blame her for wanting to be extra cautious about visitors. I would just like to have explained that to see the garden and the house from the outside would have been enough.

Tony insisted that we stay and have a cup of tea, we sat looking out at the stunning view across the hills and watched their guineafowl as they pottered around the garden. It made me realise that I miss having guineafowl, they are comical birds to keep, sadly though they can be very loud and may upset the neighbours at home. Tony was fascinated by Tom's life during the war and after, with his role at Nuremburg. We talked a lot about what it was like to live through all the unrest associated with Apartheid and how Tom had effectively gone through similar experiences during the war and having then been involved with the Trials. Tony talked about the many changes he had seen in South Africa; he had been an engineer and a lecturer in Johannesburg.

Tony mentioned that there was a gentleman's club, called the Rand Club in Johannesburg and he wondered if perhaps Tom had been a member, perhaps a way of finding someone who may have known him. I did check this out, he had never been a member. He really did keep himself to himself and lived below the radar. Auntie Betty always said that he kept himself to himself.

Jane and Tony are moving home to Ireland soon, though sadly their house is not moving very fast on the market, due to the high crime rates, political unrest and the lack of policing.

I have to admit to being upset that I did not get to see Tom's house properly, though I have walked in his footsteps, a few steps at least, seen his beautiful garden and the house from Tony and Jane's garden. I understand the issues of privacy, security and respect the owner's position. I have learned a lot about Johannesburg and what it used to be like as well as how it is now. I feel that I have a better understanding of Tom and his life here in South Africa, the life he loved, and I can certainly understand why he loved this country. It is uniquely beautiful, rich in minerals, diverse and as was once said, 'is a world in one country.' There is so much space, huge skies, opportunities, and such entrepreneurism. Auntie Bet always told me that Tom had a nice house in the mountains, and so he did. Well, his house is in the hills, and Johannesburg is a high altitude, so I will give her that. Now of course the area is very developed, so many properties, though each one seems to have a double plot. Things have changed so much over the last forty years; it is almost impossible to see exactly what it was like when Tom lived there, I wondered if it had been a gated area in his day. It would be almost sixty years now since he bought this house in the hills. To place him here, has been an important milestone for me.

Tony had filled some gaps and added both local and location history for me. There are of course many issues here in South Africa and whilst Apartheid is officially over there are many black people saying that nothing has really improved, and that Nelson Mandela would be turning in his grave if he knew what was happening. Interestingly, what I can see is the gap between the rich black people and poor black people getting bigger and more extreme and there appears to be unrest because of it. I am no politician, this is just what I have heard, been told and what I have observed, particularly in Soweto.

For Tom, being the eldest of eleven may have felt a little claustrophobic in a small town; despite being a close family. I get the feeling that Tom wanted to discover himself and set up a life apart from family. Perhaps being in the war, he found the bug for travel and anonymity. British Insulation Calendar Cables (BICC) gave him that opportunity and he took it with both hands. He travelled the world and his life ended in South Africa, his home and citizenship.

I am so grateful to Jane and Tony, for their welcome, the information, the relaxing and pleasant afternoon; for Jane answering my plea on South African Genealogy. I cannot thank them enough; without them I would have left feeling empty-handed.

Our driver had had a good nap, having parked the car under a very large shady tree. He took us to Norwood now where we had shopped on our first visit to Johannesburg, we needed to do a food shop for our trip tomorrow, when we would move on to the Mountain Sanctuary Park for a couple of days.

For our last meal at 'Fawlty Towers' there were 'takeaway' pizzas on the hot plate for us, we were told this as the owners were on their way out, Patience had the evening off. No choice, rather bland and boring pizza, no salad, no fruit, no desert.

In some ways I shall be pleased to leave Johannesburg and Pretoria area, to move away from the security fencing, armed response guards, the probability of carjacking where you are advised to give the thieves anything they demand, and the barking of guard dogs in the neighbourhood. It did not help being told that if anyone was car-jacked, if there was a woman in the car, they would be taken as well. Though I think two old ladies in their sixties, they would probably have thrown us back! Not being used to living behind bars, it did make you feel somewhat uneasy. And at the end of the day, who was being protected from whom?

We never actually felt unsafe, though there was a feeling of unease at times, not enough to stop us having a wonderful time and meeting some amazing people.

20th January

Today we leave the faded glory of the colonial residence on the outskirts of Pretoria. The owner came into the dining room just as we were finishing breakfast, cheap fish fingers, chips, blue ice-cream soda flavoured yogurt, and mouldy bread! I found it interesting that he made a point of saying that we should all get on and live together, and that he is not a racist and was brought up to accept all groups of people. Patience came in and said your breakfast is here 'baas', she was carrying a plate piled high with scrambled eggs and what looked like wholemeal cut bread as opposed to the mouldy sliced white bread in our breadbin. He said 'thank you', though he did not look at her, and her whole demeanour became submissive, her body language made her seem oppressed. She stood slightly hunched in the corner, not making eye contact with him, or Rosy and me. He talked about how terrible the situation in Zimbabwe was and how 'poor Patience had had to flee the country', but he did not include her in the conversation, or make eye contact, it was as if she was not there. She cowered in his presence. I found this quite upsetting and embarrassing as Rosy and I had engaged with Patience on several occasions, talked to her about her family, laughed with her about the pool yesterday, it was all good humoured, she had been laughing and smiling, such a different person to the woman I had just seen. Patience had a happy and sunny personality who hummed and sang as she went about her duties. I hardly recognised her in front of her 'baas'.

This whole scenario made me wonder how Tom may have been with his African servants, the British and Afrikaans, were neither particularly popular with the black community, particularly during the Apartheid and understandably so. I know that at one point there was a very heated discussion between Tom and my uncle Jim who was staying with him, it ended with a bit of a punch up I am told! Tom had specifically said that Jim was not to speak to the servants and Jim spoke to them. Tom said that this put the servants in a difficult position, should they answer and be in trouble, or not answer and appear rude? The servants were there to do their job and not to engage with visitors. At the time, perhaps this was common practise. All that I have heard about Tom suggests to me that he would have treated his servants fairly and built next to his house was a house for the servants.

Later in the morning when we were due to leave, the owner came out and asked if I had witnessed a disturbance outside the gates yesterday. It must have happened when we were out as I had not seen or heard anything. What I had seen about ten minutes earlier was the owner shouting at a young man sitting outside the security gate. The gate was opening for someone to drive in, the owner shouted, 'you, stay out, don't come in!' Apparently yesterday this same youth had been harassing Patience, he appeared to be comatose, perhaps with drink and possibly drugs. The owner had called the police to have him moved away. The police arrived quite quickly. The owner shouted for Patience and both she and the owner went down to the gate to talk to the police, Patience walking several paces behind. It seemed clear that the owner did most of the talking and Patience verified the situation. The police put the youth in the car and drove off.

Patience had stood behind her boss during the whole interaction, perhaps because she did not want to make eye contact with the youth, however as they turned to walk back up to the house, they walked side by side. Patience was chatty to her boss and he was asking if she felt better now; saying that she need not worry as 'he will not be on the streets for a very long time'. It was good to see this protection of his staff and very different body language to that of this morning at breakfast.

A few minutes before we were due to leave, the owner came out with his wife and made a big show of what he had done, and what he was going to do with the place, and was today, oozing false charm along with his wife who we had seen in passing though she had not introduced herself until now. I think they wanted a good review!

We arrived at the Mountain Sanctuary Park just after 3pm, having been taken for a quick tour of some of the prominent buildings in Pretoria, by our driver. We felt that we could not miss seeing some of the capital city. We were taken to see the Union Buildings, which we had seen from a distance yesterday and wondered what they were. The gardens there are beautiful, and we were escorted down to see the massive statue of Nelson Mandela, it really was quite magnificent. The views across the city were amazing and we had a clear view over to Proclamation Hill.

Our driver took us up to see the University of South

Africa, home to approximately 300,000 students, he was clearly and rightly very proud of this amazing architectural building. We also saw the monument at Proclamation Hill. We then set off for the mountains. We were a little worried about our driver as on leaving the Union buildings he had stopped the car at the junction, left us with the keys in the ignition and went to be sick behind a bush, the same thing happened in a layby as we set off to the mountains. Carjacking came to mind! I suggested that if he was ill, we should call Lawrence and get another driver. He did not want to do that; he had only recently started working for Lawrence. Whilst we were left at the junction an official was shouting at him to move the car.

The setting of the Mountain Sanctuary was stunning, and once again exceeded our expectations. This was Africa at close quarters, views over the plains and mountains. The log cabin was light, spacious and welcoming. The views were breathtaking. We quickly sorted ourselves out and went for a walk to find the rapids. It was quite beautiful down there, a lengthy walk and we saw and heard no one until we found the rapids, apart from the bird song which was lovely. We saw what looked like a very clear lion footprint which was a little unnerving as there are not supposed to be any lions here. Perhaps we should check with the ranger tomorrow. You are literally walking in the bush here; I was not keen to meet a lion strolling up the path to meet me! We were about two hours on our walk and felt that we should not be out and about after dark, we had already seen some baboons on arrival, so having enjoyed exploring a little we decided it was time to sort out the food shop that we had done yesterday and prepare a fresh, tasty salad for tea and a beautifully juicy, tasty melon for dessert. The fruit and vegetables are so fresh and tasty, so much bigger and brighter in colour than they are by the time we get them in the UK.

The cabin could easily sleep four people, spacious and well equipped, though no cooker there was a microwave if we had needed it. There were windows all around and they are real picture windows onto wild Africa. We had a birds-eye view from all directions, so when the midges came out in the evening, we did not miss any opportunity to see wildlife, birds or the amazing sunset. This evening we have seen a monkey and a whole family of tree squirrels chattering in the trees.

Sitting watching the sun go down and a white, bright, full moon rising was a wonderful experience, and especially so with the backdrop of mountains and bush. The pink and orange sky, the bright light of the luminous moon and a few birds singing their last songs for the day, the bats coming out and playing with the light, what an amazing end to our day. What a country.

21st January

We woke up to the noise of baboons clanging and bashing bin lids as they looked for food, unbelievably noisy. I am not a lover of baboons as they seem quite aggressive, they are fun to watch through the windows though. Three of the group shot down the path directly in front of our cabin to check out the bins closer to the swimming pool. Others played seriously rough and tumble games on the camping field behind our cabin, we could still watch through the kitchen window. And so, by 6.00am I was very wide awake. Once the baboons had moved away it became quiet and peaceful once again.

We walked down to the West Pools today, again quite a long walk and until you arrived at the pools there were no clues as to where they might be, that is apart from the map we had been given. It was about an hour's walk out there. The pools are surrounded by what look like sandstone boulders, structured into a variety of shapes and yet on closer inspection they are packed tight with tiny quartz crystals, they are also incredibly smooth and therefore slippery when wet or dry. The rock formations tower above you once you have succeeded in climbing down to the pools. When you look up, it feels as if the towers are moving due to the light reflection of the clear spring waters dancing against the rocks. I managed to capture it on video, it really looked as though the spirits from the past were dancing around the place where they had collected water and bathed hundreds, thousands of years ago.

When we initially arrived, I did not think that I would be able to climb down, mainly because I thought I would not be able to climb out. There were two guys down there when we arrived who offered to help us, we declined. After they had left however, Rosy decided to give it a try, once she had got down, I decided to have a go and was so pleased that we made it. The water was cold, cooling, and fresh, reminding me of one of my favourite places at home, Echo Lake. I had forgotten just how cold pure spring water is, in the heat of this sun though it was a delight to cool off. The setting was just magical. As I floated in the water looking up at the clear blue sky I thought of the animals and particularly the wild cats that might come here to drink, early morning and evenings. Was there a cat watching us right now perhaps? I also thought very briefly about snakes that might be around but decided to bin that thought.

We had almost two hours of absolute bliss, sun, peace, perfect surroundings, birdsong, and beautiful butterflies, all to ourselves; at which point two groups of youngsters arrived and whilst they were great fun, we decided to leave then to it and make the climb up the boulders to walk back to the cabin. We will visit again tomorrow. It was a hot walk back as it was now nearly 2.00pm.

I sat on the veranda, writing my journal, admiring the deep blue sky, the expanse of lush green African bush, Africa just spreading herself out in front of us, sharing her beauty. The birds were singing, so many different tunes, tending to sing solo as I have noticed before, and every so often you hear a screech of an animal in the bush, the breeze is light and full of mystery. Suddenly there will be a big gust of wind which dies almost as soon as it begins. Dry heat, red dust, bright green plants, this is Africa.

In the evening we went for a walk down to the swimming pool and caught sight of a pair of mongoose stalking two pigeons. One of the groups of youngsters were walking along the path and both the pigeons and the mongoose disappeared. Many of the bushes look as though they have been burnt; they look like charcoal. Apparently, it is that they have been so parched of water that they die off and when the rains return, they start to sprout new growth. I saw a large bird, a hornbill with a large black bill sitting in the tree in front of the cabin this evening. It was brown and black in colour with a huge curved black beak, so quiet I nearly missed it, interestingly it seems, in all countries, to be the small birds that sing the loudest songs.

This truly was a sanctuary of peace and tranquillity. Even the swimming pool had panoramic views of the bush. Later in the evening we were entertained by a family of tree squirrels. A mother trying to teach her tiny baby to jump from the tree onto our roof. Mum kept rushing up the tree with the baby behind her, she would then jump onto the roof, but every time, the baby would stop and then tear off down the tree trunk and wait for its mother to tempt it again, chattering encouragingly all the time. This happened about six times in quick succession and then I think the mother decided that was enough training for one evening.

We saw scrub hares this evening, they were huge, standing

on all fours, they were bigger than a large domestic cat, by a long way. We saw a ground-scraper thrush and by about 7.30pm everything went quiet outside. The bats came out and darted around the trees and the eaves of our roof, that was my cue to go indoors. In daylight you felt like you were a million miles from civilisation and yet at night there was a reminder from the twinkling lights of towns or cities a long way in the distance.

22nd January

A beautiful day, amazing sharp light. It had been quite a noisy night one way and another, there were a group of about fifteen students, some of whom we met at the pools yesterday. They were out and about in the bush with torches, shouting, whooping and generally having fun until after the silence hour of 9.00pm, by 9.30pm everything was quiet. The birdlife that seemed to have been stunned into silence by the students now began their choral salute of the day, each with their solo rendition and then silence, apart from a few bumps and bangs, possibly squirrels still having night flight training on our roof and perhaps the baboons were having a midnight snack from the bins. There was a lot of rustling, which I chose to ignore and there was a huge translucent moon risen to its full height lighting up the bush with its led light. It looked beautiful and yet of course these nights were a poacher's delight.

The next morning, I woke at about 6.00am again and

went to sit out on the veranda, overlooking the African bush. The light luminous, the sky bright, soil red and trees of varying colours of green and then the charcoal branches. The birdsong was loud, though not like a dawn chorus that we hear at home. I was sitting quite comfortably taking a photograph of a crested barbet and I heard a loud bang, then another and assumed that the baboons were back around the campsite, though I realised that there was no chatter going on which I have noticed from baboons before. I became aware of a slight noise to my right and as I turned, saw two vervet monkeys sitting on our bin, they were empty and so not their lucky day. I took a photo and then out of the corner of my eye I saw the rest of the troop, or barrel of monkeys walking up the ramp towards our veranda. I have to admit to jumping quickly out of my chair, grabbing my mug and camera and making a dash for the door, closing it very quickly behind me! As I looked, I saw one of the larger monkeys creeping out from under the table another running along the railing. A mother with two babies shot across the veranda and into the tree. Apart from running along the veranda and jumping on and off our roof, they were in the tree for about two hours. And yes, I had been watching them from indoors!

The younger ones were now getting to be 'cheeky monkeys' and were playing hide and seek with us as we draw back curtains. The noise of them jumping up and down on the veranda and the table is difficult to describe and yet, unless they have a disagreement between themselves, they are incredibly light-footed and quiet, unlike the heavy-footed baboons.

Once the monkeys had realised, we were not going to feed them and they had played themselves out, they disappeared around the side of our cabin and moved over to the next cabin, or perhaps off back to their particular tree where they live. They seem to travel long distances and I expect that were on route to somewhere else, they have realised that sometimes they can find easy pickings from the bins. When they had all left, we were no longer trapped in the cabin! Neither of us wanted to be in too close contact to the monkeys despite the fascination in watching them. They do bite and carry ticks, best to be watched from a safe distance.

We went off for our walk towards the West Pools, we were slightly later today, about 10.30am and the sun was already high, hot, and beautiful. We missed one of the paths on the way and ended up having to climb over the red rocks studded with tiny quartz crystals in order to return to the right path. Always considering what may be lurking in the undergrowth or indeed sunning themselves on the rocks. We saw a beautifully bright coloured grasshopper today, well that is what I thought it was. We spent a wonderful two hours at the pools, totally alone, listening to the birds, watching dragonflies and if we were being watched it was by silent creatures.

The water, still cooling and fresh, the reflections continuing to dance up and down the columns of rock and the green, leafy bushes nearby, like the spirits of old, guarding this magical place. The weaver birds were darting in and out of the bush having collected seed and flying off to feed their young, we did not see any of their nests here, they must be further down towards the rapids, given their direction of flight.

After two hours of sun, silence, and soothing water we were thinking about making a move, when we heard another group of youngsters heading our way. They told us of other pools they had found further up the ravine, deeper and bigger, though difficult to access, we decided best not try that, we had managed to get up and down to these without injury and thought we would leave it at that. We still have so many adventures ahead of us.

We walked back to the cabin, to relax on the balcony, a beautiful shady spot during the heat of the afternoon. As we walked back Rosy shouted 'mind your back' with a level of anxiety in her voice that made me turn around immediately. I looked back, there was nothing there, though I had also heard a weird sound, like that of large flapping wings. We both stood still. Rosy was convinced that she had heard an ATV or quad bike coming behind her, and yet we both realised the path was not wide enough to accommodate one. I thought I had heard a large bird of prey swooping low behind me. In fact, it was a random gust of wind, that had come up the valley and through the trees with great speed and purpose. At least that is what we chose to believe.

Whilst I was sitting writing this, I experienced the same thing again, the wind of African spirits perhaps. Once you have experienced it, it is less scary, though somewhat spooky, it is sudden and short, so quick that you do not notice anything move with it, just the extreme noise from the gust, not even the red dust blows. Was it spooky or magical, perhaps both, we were in the bush after all and about an hour from a town and further from any city?

I could see for miles sitting on this balcony, bush and plains. I could hear voices from the swimming pool when the wind carried them my way. I could not see another cabin, or a person. I have said it before, this Mountain Sanctuary Park was truly a sanctuary, a writer's paradise, a real jewel to visit and experience. Perhaps we were feeling the atmosphere more acutely having been in Johannesburg and Pretoria, with all the issues about security. This was pure bliss.

We enjoyed a few hours of writing, and reading books about South Africa, where people had visited places that we have been, also touring off the beaten track. This evening we walked down to the man-made swimming pool. We had a good time, Rosy swimming and me floating about, following doctor's orders. We were still in the pool when one of the maintenance team turned up, he was carrying a box. He knelt down lifted a hatch and proceeded to undo the bottle top. At that point I suggested to Rosy that we get out, quickly. He had not told us what he was doing and had not asked us to get out of the pool, we have noticed that most staff did not make eye contact or speak until we had spoken to them and this seems to be a rule across the board.

As we got out, he had begun pouring this whole bottle of bright yellow liquid into the workings, perhaps chlorine, I was not sure. He then opened a very large 5 litre bottle of a bright green substance and walked around the pool pouring all of the contents into the pool. Rosy thought perhaps this one was a disinfectant solution. The pool was well maintained and clean, though I did not really want to be in it when all the solutions were being added. It was quite clear that the job would have been done whether we were in the pool or not.

I had trouble getting out of the pool, due to my hip and put my foot on the grass to balance myself and caught sight of something black, about three inches long scooting into the wall, perhaps a scorpion, not very sensible move on my part.

When we returned to the cabin, having sat on the sunbeds to dry off first; we had to get ourselves organised to leave in the morning. We packed our bags, finished up food that we had in the fridge, leaving enough fruit for breakfast. We will be returning to Johannesburg in the morning in order to take the train to Cape Town.

I felt sorry to be saying goodbye to this beautiful place, it epitomised the African landscape, the quiet, the expanse, the wonderful colours and sounds of the bush, though it is always best to leave wanting more.

We sat and watched the bats ducking and diving about the trees and under the veranda eaves and roof. I am not keen on bats; it stems back to when I was at school and I had very long hair. We used to walk up the drive sometimes at dusk and people would say that the bats would get into your hair and you can't get them out! I know; but it just comes back to me every time I see bats, even though my hair is so much shorted now. Bats are fascinating to watch, from indoors.

Last minute jobs, charging phones and cameras with difficulty as we did not have the correct adapters with us. We have not had internet whilst we have been here, and I alerted the family back home that they would not hear from us for a couple of days. I need to call Lawrence to ensure that our driver will be here at 11.00am to collect us in the morning and I do hope he is feeling better now as we have a longer journey back to Johannesburg.

Tomorrow our adventure continues in a new direction.

23rd January

An exciting start to the day. At about 7.30am I spotted a herd of kudu across the valley, initially thinking they were cows until we looked through the telephoto lens on the camera and through binoculars. The rising sun was shining on their backs and showing a wonderful copper colour along with the flash of white in the stripes on their backs and face. It was difficult to say how many there were as they were moving towards the trees down on the plain, I would guess between fifteen and twenty. We watched them for some time, and they seemed to slow as they found shade around the trees and I imagine the river running down from the pools where we have been bathing.

As usual for that time of day, the various birds were singing and two large hornbills flew over the cabin, making an amazing squawking noise, their shadows like pterodactyls, perhaps they are descendants. I had managed to get a photograph of a hornbill yesterday as it stopped to rest in the tree in front of the cabin.

Two of the baboon troop had just rummaged through the campsite behind the cabin only to be disappointed that the bins were empty, no campers last night. They must have headed off for other pickings as we did not see them again. The scrub hare had been to visit this morning, seemingly alone and we have had no monkeys to play hide and seek with today.

Just before 9.00am Rosy noticed two white trucks driving in the direction of where we had seen the kudu. The second truck had a trailer and about ten minutes later we heard three shots fired. It may be that the herd needed to be culled, or that people just needed food to eat, or perhaps it was poachers, though I think it was all too obvious in broad daylight to be poachers. With the big white moon, we have had for the last couple of nights it would have been perfect poaching conditions, the skies lit up by the moon as the sun lights up the day.

I asked one of the rangers about trophy hunting when we were at Pilansberg National Park. I have always been against it, yet he explained to me that the parks that allow trophy hunting; only hunt old or sick animals and that the money then comes back to the park and can then be used for the upkeep of the younger fitter animals. He said that these particular animals would need to be put down or culled sooner rather than later and that the money that came in, is essential for care of the existing animals and the cost of the anti-poaching teams. I could understand that explanation and I no longer felt so cross when I see images of these animals with their hunters displayed on social media and such, in fact it makes you realise that these people posing as big game hunters are maybe not quite so clever as they think. It saddens me to see any animal killed, though now , I have a better understanding of why this continues to happen.

We have seen beautiful birds, insects, huge amber coloured dragonflies, yellow and orange along with yellow-pansy butterflies, elephant hawk moths, a brightly coloured poisonous grasshopper, and enormous hornets during our stay here, along with all the amazing animals. The scenery, pools and rapids have been stunning, and the location better than I could ever have hoped for, Africa spread out before our eyes, now though, it was time to leave, continue our adventure and return to Johannesburg for one night.

We had a two-and-a-half-hour drive back to the city. Our driver was not very communicative today, perhaps he was embarrassed about having been ill when he drove us here, or perhaps he thought I may have contacted his boss about the situation the other day. He drove very fast in places and was constantly looking down at his telephone, it did not feel safe. I felt that I should call Lawrence, his boss. The difficulty was that a great many people drive fast here, and frequently using their mobile phones as well. Whilst I believe health and safety can at times be totally over the top, it is interesting how it feels in a country that does not appear to adhere to a health and safety regime at all.

As we have seen before, there were hawkers at junctions and traffic lights selling their wares and with their label or boards asking for money to feed their families, though once again, they were not pushy, simply hopeful and a desperate look on their faces and their demeanour. I also reflected on what Jeffrey had told us about the sellers on one side of the road being illegal immigrants from Zimbabwe and how the other side of the road would be local traders. Each aware of the situation and the needs of each other from both sides. So long as no one crosses the line, all is well.

Finally, we reach our hotel back in Johanessburg. The hotel seems fine, again better than expected given the price. Once again, we were allocated a double room, despite having sent a specific message about having a twin room. Once we were sorted out, we were on the sixth floor looking down on lots of busy people bustling about, to and from meetings, in their offices and rushing along the streets. They say that people come to Johannesburg to make money. Certainly, in this area that would ring true, it seemed to be the business centre, I think that was the reason that Tom chose to live here, though he travelled all over Africa for his work and to make his fortune.

We caught up with messages and checked in with family as we have been without Wi-Fi and will be again whilst on the train to Cape Town. I have sent a few pictures from the Mountain Sanctuary Park so that they can see what we have been up to. It is wonderful to be able to stay in touch and let the family know that we are safe and well.

We ventured up to the roof top, to see the breath-taking views over the city. With the clear sky and the pale buildings, it really was quite picturesque. I wanted to get some photographs before the light went and before the usual thunder and lightning began. As it did about two hours later.

We booked our taxi for 8.00am to ensure that we were at the railway station in plenty of time for our train, the Shosholoza Meyl to Cape Town and then went down to the restaurant for tea. Over tea we talked about all the things we have seen and done since we arrived just fourteen days ago. I cannot believe we have experienced so much; everything has been better, and more, than I could have hoped for, despite the year of planning and risk assessing.

We ate a very good tea in the hotel and paid just over £10 for the two of us including Rosy's glass of wine and the tip. We had spicy rice, mixed vegetables, sweet potato, butternut squash, yams, salsa, beetroot to share. It was delicious.

What I noticed whilst having our tea and people

watching, there were few obese black men and once again no white people walking the streets even in this business area of Johannesburg. People walk for miles in this country and it clearly helps to keep them fit and trim. We have noticed how far the children walk to school; in Pilansberg area they were already walking to school by 5.55am because of the distances. You see people walking along the side of motorways, across fields where you can see no dwellings at all. Walking is clearly a common mode of getting where you need to be.

People in the country seem to have the will and determination to get to work, to school, or to their trading post. People were collecting recycling and taking huge dumpy bags full of it to the recycling centres where they will get paid a few rand for their efforts. They are bent over, pushing trolleys loaded with dumpy bags up steep hills to get those few rand to feed their children. I salute their determination, their energy, their get up, and, do it for themselves. I cannot see that same determination happening in many people at home.

We ended the day with an amazing thunder and lightning show, I shall always think of Johannesburg when we have storms at home.

24th January

Though apparently this city never sleeps, last night was much quieter than I had expected, at least until 4.00am. I was expecting sirens to be ringing most of the night, given the crime rates in Johannesburg. We enjoyed a good spread for breakfast and found our taxi just after 8.00am to set off to Park station.

On the way to the station from the hotel it felt as if we were travelling through tunnels of time, and poverty. The streets lined with green trees and bushes turned very quickly to derelict buildings, damaged buildings, rubbish, people hoping for custom in their temporary trading posts, tyre houses, mechanic shops and various other trades. We then came to the street traders, selling cold drinks, hot drinks, fruit and vegetables, leather goods, making breakfast to go, on a braai (BBQ). Those traders, hoping to catch people on their way to work with their 'pop up shops' which seemed to be very temporary and probably constructed early in the morning. Inter-mingled, there were people who had clearly slept rough overnight, with only a piece of cardboard wrapped around them or a piece of cloth for comfort.

The office workers were in stark contrast to those plying their wares and of course this was a similar picture to other cities across the world. The gap between rich and poor seemed to be increasing within these tunnels. Lads are standing in the middle of the roads and junctions, selling sweets, fruit, and cold drinks. Some with posters saying 'hungry man, no job' and 'can't feed my family', begging, telling people of their plight and desperation. There was genuine sadness, fear, anxiety in their eyes. People were wrestling with loads of recycling goods that they had found in the bins, and cardboard that they had found outside shops. And yes, it appeared that some had spent their few rand on alcohol and, or drugs, some just seem forlorn, lost, so very sad and dejected. It is hard to see this level of poverty all around you, we had seen it in rural areas as well as towns and cities though here it was more extreme. We saw a lot of women carrying laundry bags on their heads, as we have seen in many villages and with babies in their slings on their backs, a special closeness with their mothers, watching the world go by. Not a push chair or pram in sight.

Rural areas are different, and the poverty it was not so evident with the smaller populations. Some of the rural people were farm workers, or small holders themselves, and are perhaps in a better position to put food on their table.

The driver was insistent that he should walk us down to the Premier Class lounge, we were grateful for that. Sitting in the lounge, I felt, not guilty, but not good, food was continuously bought out for us, despite the fact that most of us had eaten a hotel breakfast already today. There was fruit, sandwiches, chocolate cake, nuts, cheese and biscuits, meats, bottled water, tea and coffee available in vast amounts. Yes, I did have a piece of cheese, some nuts, and a bottle of water, but what I wanted to do was to take plates of it outside to those people who were hanging around the station, in need of sustenance. I wondered what happened to food that was left over once we boarded the train. There would have been enough to feed several families.

We were being served lunch at 12.30 on the train and yes, I know that we had paid for our tickets and all this is part of the deal. For me it felt immoral, because I had just witnessed the hardship of those people outside of this station. I suppose it simply continues to widen that gap, between having and not having. When I have those feelings, I find myself wondering what Tom would have thought and how did he look after his staff at home and at work.

We had another half an hour before boarding the train and I was pleased that we had this lounge in which to wait. I admit to having felt quite vulnerable when we walked from the taxi into the station. With no white people walking on the streets and few even driving cars in the city, we do stick out rather. We saw one white chap walking across the street from our hotel, he had an angle grinder in one hand and a box of tools in the other, clearly going to do a job. Despite the taxi driver walking us through the station to the lounge, all eyes seemed to be on us, though no one behaved in a threatening way at all. I suspect that the other passengers had felt the same, as we were all white, except for a lady from the Philippines. There were a couple of white South African passengers. Some of our fellow travellers had flown into Johannesburg and come straight to the station to catch the train.

One gentleman has done this trip seven times, that seemed quite a good recommendation. People who had visited Cape Town before were happy to share their experiences and advice with those of us visiting for the first time. We finally boarded the train and at that point, everything was as advertised. We were travelling in a blue train, though not 'The Blue train!' We were informed that we would arrive late at Cape Town due to the work taking place on the points, on the lines.

As we travelled out of Johannesburg, I felt sad that I had not found out more about Tom and also wondered if he had pulled out of Johannesburg in the direction of Cape Town as we were doing. We travelled through very different areas, we saw people walking along beside the tracks, perhaps going home, perhaps on their way to visit, or to work. We saw a herd of dairy cattle between Randfontein and Carltonville, I think they may have been Ayrshires, perhaps the herd that Jeffrey mentioned to us. Philip may be interested. For all the cows and beef stock I have seen, I did not have my camera poised for the dairy cattle!

We were served a good three course lunch as we slowly made our way towards Cape Town, the scenery was interesting and more changeable than I had expected or been led to believe. We declined afternoon tea as we really had eaten more than enough, especially as we were sitting still for most of the time, unlike our quite energetic days at the Mountain Sanctuary Park. We stayed in our cabin and watched for the wildlife instead. We were happy watching the yellow mongoose and ground squirrels running around the red rocks, earth, and grassy hillocks during an hour of standing still again. It was good to see wildlife running about in such a barren, and what could at first sight appear to be, an animal free area.

We had an interesting day, having left Johannesburg on time, had a steady ride through suburbs, townships, country-side and industrial areas. Watched the enormous goldmine slacks disappear behind us. We had been warned before we left that there may be delays due to signal work, so we were prepared. However, we were not expecting to breakdown so many times and for long periods of time. The day was particularly hot and so with no air conditioning and no ability to open windows there was a potential problem. I was pleased that we had been in the country for a couple of weeks to get acclimatised. It was the electrical issues that stopped the air conditioning from working on this hot day. Apparently, this all happens quite frequently in hot weather! The electric goes off, we stop! This happened about five times, with about five minutes of movement between each stop we were stationary for anything from ten minutes to one hour or more. However, we were told that the problem was fixed, although I think the heat had reduced with the time of day, rather than anything being properly fixed! We continued for two and a half hours, before stopping again. The plan was to limp on until we reached Kimberley at about midnight, they would change one of the two engines and then limp on again, though perhaps at a slightly quicker rate to Beaufort West to change the second engine.

The staff seemed to have coped very well in what were clearly frustrating circumstances. It was quite clear though, that this was not the first time this has happened. It must be particularly difficult for the chef, and tea was at least an hour late. I had the feeling that some of the passengers were complaining about a few issues. The tea however was good and presented well. With the electric off again, the staff were having to hand wash dishes and struggling with glasses, and so apologetic that they did not always have the correct glasses for wine, beer etc. It was not an issue on our table, though we noticed a few mutterings from others. We had emergency lighting, and with the scenery and the clear white moon it rather added to the ambiance.

The sunset had been quite astounding and Rosy had managed to capture it in some good photographs; I did not seem to be able to focus my camera properly this evening. If tea had been on time, we may have missed the spectacular display of colours and a blood orange canvas stretched across the vast African Sky.

By 9.30pm we had had enough excitement for the day and tried to settle down in our comfortable beds back in our cabin. We were quite relaxed and ready for a good night's sleep, when the train decided to stop again with a bad version of a violin concerto of squealing brakes. How much sleep would we have tonight? Rosy was prepared with her ear plugs and I was just hopeful!

We set out to have an adventure and we are certainly

having a magnificent adventure. However not everyone is taking it in their stride, and some were definitely, not amused!

25th January

I woke at 2.45am, we were stationary and in Kimberley, having arrived somewhat later than planned. At 5.15am we started to move just as the sun was rising over the diamond mines with all their engine houses and paraphernalia. The light was beautiful with pinks, oranges, mauves layered across the town and illuminating the slack piles. The town was substantial and rambled on for quite a while before we rolled into the open bush again – and surprise, we stopped again about seventeen minutes later.

As we awaited the next event on our adventurous journey, we enjoyed the view, from the comfort of our beds, watching the sunrise was pretty amazing and as Philip has already said, not something I see very often. The world was completely still, not a blade of grass moving, nor a leaf on the trees as the sun lit up the vast Karoo.

At around 9.00am we crossed over the Orange River, the longest river in South Africa, it is a valuable resource to the country. It is always a surprise when the landscape changes dramatically from the arid interior to a wide, fast flowing river. We have passed mine workers houses, now derelict and what seemed to have been substantial houses that appeared to be in good condition, just left desolate. Did people struggle to make a living here or was it that the industries that had thrived, dried up like some of the riverbeds and the people just upped sticks and moved on?

At this stage of our journey, we were running fourteen hours late and would not get into Cape Town until late in the evening. We had a full day of armchair sight-seeing and a second evening on the train with ample supplies of food and water. The train manager was so surprised and happy when we said that we were quite content. Thankfully, we had not made any commitments in Cape Town and would simply arrive later than expected, not a complete surprise given some of the reviews we had read. There were people who had flights booked for early tomorrow morning and were not happy and so a bus was organised to collect anyone who wanted to leave the train at Beaufort West, to bus them down to Cape Town, with I might add, security guards as escort. About half of the passengers opted for the bus though most of our carriage were staying put. The bus ride would be at least six hours and my view was that we had paid and booked to be on the train, and we were happy to finish our journey as arranged. The train manager announced that lunch would be served at 1pm, in theory we should have disembarked in Cape Town at 12.30pm.

I contacted Eric, our Airbnb host and he kindly said that whatever time we arrived he would collect us from the station, he did not want us to be waiting for a taxi late at night or early morning. This journey had been everything, and more that I had hoped for, we have seen a variety of wildlife which we were not really expecting to see in such a parched area. We have seen sheep, cattle and donkeys on the domestic front and then much to my delight I have spotted wildebeests, impala, steenbok, bush buck, an African harrier hawk, angora goats, white wallabies or kangaroos, they were even more of a surprise, and no I was not dreaming. The gentleman sharing our table for meals saw them to! I saw what looked like an eagle, it had a brown back with white striped wings, we passed reed beds and saw the sacred African ibis, a herd of springbok as well as the occasional loners. I also saw either the black chested snake eagle or the African hawk eagle, the snake eagle was probably the most likely, given the area. I say that I saw these animals, Rosy saw some of them as well, though not all. When the train was moving it was difficult as by the time you saw them, they were gone and so not always time to say 'look'. Rosy is still not convinced that I saw white kangaroos!

Having been told that lunch would be served at 1pm, at 12.45pm the train manager came to tell us that the staff were not prepared to serve lunch as they had not been paid their overtime for five months, they had had enough. Bearing in mind we were already fourteen hours late. We were told that we could stay on the train until 7am, but we would have no food or water and therefore we may prefer to disembark at Beaufort West. We sadly packed our bags and sat waiting for arrival at Beaufort West. I was not looking forward to the bus ride. I prefer to be able to get up and walk around to loosen my hip, Rosy is the same with her back. Another important consideration was, if all the staff are on strike, who was managing the security issues? We were due into Beaufort West at 4pm.

During the last two hours heading towards Beaufort West, a lady travelling with a group, planned to phone ahead to order pizzas and bottles of water, for those of us who wished to stay aboard the train. We added our order.

Just after 2pm, we had another message from the train manager saying that finally the strike was over, and the staff had been paid. I have to say I was in sympathy with the staff and could understand why they had to put their foot down. The minimum wage here is just R16 which is just under £1. We were served lunch. The passengers who opted for the bus were duly sent on their way at Beaufort West and we were there for about half an hour which gave people the option of getting off the train and stretching their legs. Despite the strike having been averted, some of the staff were not happy to offer further service and so we organised our own beds, ate what we were offered, continued to drink water and enjoyed the view.

In theory the strike had abated, we set off from Beaufort West with a lighter train as about half of the passengers had continued their journey by bus. I was so pleased that we could continue by train.

Seeing the Karoo really put the size of this wonderful country into perspective. I could see the Karoo stretching away for miles towards mountainous terrain in all directions.

Whilst the terrain was arid and harsh, we had already seen so many animals and birds, so unexpected given what I have read and been told. Barren, grey and parched as it was, there were still surprises. Some oasis appears from nowhere, dried riverbeds crossing under the railway tracks and then suddenly a huge area of green grass, luxurious grass feeding a flock of sheep. Derelict houses and homesteads, scattered and abandoned throughout this harsh landscape. Then suddenly out of nowhere a banded mongoose and a white headed grey bodied heron. The Orange River clearly supplied the water for irrigation of grassland and fruit trees along the way.

The end of our journey on the Shosholza Premiere Class train, Johannesburg to Cape Town was nearly over. It had been eventful and interesting. The scenery stunning, the light and sunsets beautiful. Yes, there had been trials and tribulations with break downs, strikes and a record-breaking delay of twenty hours. However, I personally would do it all over again.

I was concerned that reviews following this particular trip and other issues in the past, may at some point result in this wonderful opportunity and adventure being cancelled. That would be a terrible shame and I would like to say that the staff were amazing, they were smiling and efficient and they needed to let their company know that enough was enough. I would recommend this journey to everyone, with the proviso that you do not have important connections or events awaiting you at Cape Town.

I spoke to one of the South African travellers who brought visitors on this train regularly, and asked her what her thoughts were, she had the same concerns as I had for the service of this train. She sent me this blog account with permission to include it in my journal and when writing this book.

Gail wrote:

January

Once again, we drove to Park Station and dropped off our rental car, which is easy and safe. Otherwise, I would suggest using Uber.

Premier Class has a secure lounge in the station concourse. And we were back on the train to Cape town.

After lunch, we were told the train was running late, but that we would be getting a new locomotive in Kimberly. We just enjoyed a glass of wine and a nap. Dinner came and went, and we lost track of where we were or how delayed the train was. We slept so well. By breakfast though, it was clear that the train was way behind schedule, and we were offered a coach ride from Beaufort West to Cape Town or the option of staying on the train another night. Most people in our half of the train opted to stay, as long as drinks were available, and meals would be served. This involved a lot of calling ahead to change arrangements with hotels, car rental companies and friends. But everyone remained pretty relaxed. When the kitchen staff downed tools due to non-

payment of overtime, I rallied a few troops with a plan to order take -out pizzas and have them delivered to the Beaufort West station. Luckily, the "strike" was quickly averted, and meal service re- commenced. We all clapped and cheered when we reached Beaufort West. We watched the other passengers schlepping off to the bus for a six-hour drive to Cape Town, but we just cracked open another bottle of wine. The camaraderie in our dining car was festive and we met passengers from Brazil, Holland, Guyana and the UK. I don't know if we got another locomotive there or not, but we made it to Maatjiesfontein by dusk. After dinner, we settled in for the second night. Somewhere on the outskirts of Cape Town, the train pulled into a siding for a few hours, the plan being getting us into the station and all off the train by 7am.

It's hard to explain how so much inconvenience can actually be that enjoyable! It certainly was an African adventure. We will definitely do it again, with flexible arrival plans in place.

Come on PRASA, get your house in order. Fix this before your reputation is ruined for good. The Premier Class Train to Cape Town is a real gem of a train journey for tourists! We have done overnight train journeys in Australia, the US, Europe and SE Asia and we still highly recommend this journey for value for money, comfort and enjoyment.

However, if punctuality is your only concern though, take a flight!

For my part as well, I do hope that the train continues with this service, it is a wonderful way to see the interior of this amazing country.

26th January

We eventually arrived in Cape Town, just after 4.15am, we had slept well considering the rather noisy and bumpy ride given the mountain pass and the points. We seemed to have the noisiest of brakes. We got ourselves packed and organised to depart the train at 7.00am as arranged, at this point we had been left on a siding to be returned to the platform at 7.00am. The staff who were wanting a quick turnaround and with the hope of perhaps nipping home for a couple of hours were very keen to move us on, and when we pulled back into the station at about 6.00am they were keen that we should vacate. Luckily everyone stood their ground, we had been advised not to leave the train before 7.00am and our Airbnb host Eric, had kindly agreed to collect us at 7.00am. As we walked through the station, we saw a handbag with its contents strewn across the platform, perhaps the thief was interrupted, or perhaps it fell off a pile of luggage. Who knows, it looked a bit suspect and I was pleased that we were going to be collected.

As we had already missed our first half-day and night in Cape Town, Eric and his wife, kindly provided breakfast for us and we sat out under the tree enjoying fresh air and sunshine, there were a pair of ibis in the tree and they were feeding a youngster. Suddenly everything seemed calm and we felt ready to continue our adventures and to have fresh air and exercise, which we had missed on the train. We wasted no time in booking a taxi to take us to where we could collect the cable car to go up to Table Mountain.

It was glorious up at the top, a slight breeze, certainly not the wind that we had been warned about. The sky was blue, the views stunning, though there was smoke drifting across from the wildfires that had been popping up during the drought. The cable car had been closed for three days due to high winds and so today we are lucky. We had a packed itinerary, and due to the delays with the train, only three full days in Cape Town to visit the places on our list, Table Mountain, Robben Island, the Penguins at Boulders Beach, plus other adventures if time allowed.

We walked around the designated paths and saw wonderful views over Cape Town and over to Robben Island, as well as fauna and flora. We saw several daasies, similar looking to large guinea-pigs though actually related to the elephant, according to the literature, its real name is a rock hyrax.

We walked for quite a while, amazing how big the top of the mountain was, and then there were lots of gullies and nooks and crannies to explore. It was a little worrying to see people climbing right out to the edge in order to have their photo taken, one leg in the air, balancing on a pinnacle; it looked very precarious, though there was also something good about not having fences everywhere and leaving people to use their common sense about danger, which was quite liberating. We spent about three hours up on the mountain and then bought a few postcards to send home.

The cable car had a revolving floor, enabling everyone to get a great view of the journey up and down, both of which only lasted three minutes. The view was breath-taking. I managed to video our descent which will be kept as a great reminder of a wonderful experience.

People were abseiling from the top of the mountain, there were also a lot of people who had climbed up to the top, rather than taking the cable car. From our accommodation we had an excellent view of the mountain, we were at the base. We could see the cable car and whether it was in operation and our host apparently frequently walks about a third of the way up the mountain for exercise. He did ask if we would like to join him, we politely declined!

On our descent we asked the taxi to take us home via the supermarket so that we could do our food shop. He took us to Woolworths, the closest shop to our accommodation, we stocked up for a few days, so that we could have good fresh salads and take picnics as appropriate, such beautiful places to sit and contemplate. We booked the taxi for 9.00am the next morning.

In the afternoon, I read for an hour or so and then fell asleep for a couple of hours, we had not had a great deal of sleep on the train, though we had had plenty of excitement! We had lovely fresh salad for our tea, which has become a regular pattern for us. We wrote post cards and then read, followed by a good night's sleep.

Due to the drought that Cape Town has been suffering,

we are being very careful with water and doing our washing as we showered, catching water from the shower in a bucket and using it for the loo. It is important that we all take responsibility for saving as much water as possible.

27th January

Having had a comfortable and quiet night, we had breakfast and set off to meet our taxi, which did not arrive. We thought we were going to have similar experiences to using uber, so I rang the company to ask where they were and was told that you cannot book the taxi without ringing the company, so I re-booked and within about twenty minutes a different driver arrived, very apologetic for leaving us standing in the sun, he seemed quite perplexed when we said that we were enjoying the heat.

Whilst waiting for the taxi, we realised as we looked up, that the cable car was not in operation today, that did not bode well for our boat trip out to Robben Island. The taxi dropped us near where the ferry left for the island and told us to give him a call if we wanted to go somewhere instead. Robben Island was cancelled for the day, so we transferred the tickets over to tomorrow and went to plan B. We called the cab and went out to the airport to hire a car, meaning that we would be able to get ourselves back to the airport easily for our departure in a couple of days.

Our taxi driver insisted on walking with us into the airport and pointing us in the direction of car hire. There was a steel band playing just outside the main entrance with a group of dancers, what a lovely welcome to Cape Town people would have, following a tiring flight. We picked up the hire car and set off down the coast to Boulders Beach. The scenery was stunning all the way down, passing through towns and villages with a wide range of architecture from colonial style buildings to ultra-modern condos. We followed a truck for some time, there was a washing machine on the back along with a family, eight children of varying ages and two men. They were smiling and laughing to us and I held up my camera to see if I could take a photo, they smiled with a thumbs up and one of the men put his tongue out, all good humoured. What a truck full of happy people, they pulled into a car park along the beach front, perhaps they were going to have a day out before returning home with their new purchase.

We spent a wonderful day at Boulders Beach, I was so pleased that we opted for the hire car rather than taking an organised trip. We saw about six bus-loads of people come and go; they did not have a lot of time to spend watching these comical penguins. From one initial pair of these endangered African penguins, there are now over two thousand, thanks to this amazing sanctuary. Whilst we were on boardwalks, we were almost within touching distance to the penguins as they go about their business, nesting, mating, incubating eggs, raising their young and swimming in the open sea.

Some of the areas where you can swim and picnic, the penguins just wandered about the beach. Apparently, they do bite if feeling threatened and so like most animals it is best to observe and let them choose how close they come to you. There were young chicks still with their mothers, expectant fathers standing over the nests, eggs were being turned, nests were being dug in the sand. Some penguins were moulting and last year's hatch still a brownish colour. The noise they make is just like a donkey braying, hence their nickname 'Jackass' penguins.

The wind was very strong, the sand was blowing, and as we were wearing shorts, our legs felt like they were being sand-blasted, my hair felt like wire-wool, again, and people were losing hats, pashminas and several belongings blown onto the beach. We had the most amazing day watching the penguins in their territory, enjoying the ocean, and being protected. I was amused however when I heard someone say, 'so how do they keep them in'. The penguins are native and wild, we are the ones in the enclosure to afford us the privilege of observing them in their natural habitat.

We saw the penguins under trees and nesting in the manmade nests provided for them, however mostly they were digging out their own nests and being very independent of what had been set up for them.

We enjoyed a very scenic drive back to Cape Town crossing the peninsular and drove through Chapman's Peak Drive, the scenery was amazing, the beaches of white sand

and turquoise sea with sand blasting on your skin as you walked across. The wind was blowing a 'hooley' and Rosy nearly lost her hold on the car door with the ferocity of the gusts off the sea.

We saw windsurfers, having an amazing time, jumping and turning as the light started to drop over the sea. The colours of their sails stood out in the glimmering light. As well as penguins, we have encountered families of dassies, enjoyed wonderful scenery, met friendly people and all in all had a brilliant day out.

We found Glencoe Road and our accommodation without too much trouble, we had hoped to stop at Signal Point on the way back to catch the last of the setting sun, though there were police blockades, we now know that the wild fires were still burning from Lions Head down to Signal Point. We will have to take that off our list and hope for the people living near-by that the fires die out soon.

Cape Town is a very cosmopolitan city and without the presence of Table Mountain and Robben Island, it could easily be anywhere in the world. It is an exceptionally clean city and has interesting architecture. The Waterfront complex is very plush and inviting to both locals and tourists. Unlike Johannesburg people feel safe here, people walk about the streets and shops with an air of confidence. Like all cities it has its areas where you should not wander about at any time, and like all cities it is best not to become complacent. We have enjoyed it all and felt very safe. Having said that, I reiterate that we had not felt threatened in Johannesburg, and generally people were very helpful, we followed advice and did not put ourselves at risk. The only place where I had felt uncomfortable was walking into Park Station, though perhaps that was my embarrassment at the poverty people are living with, rather than any action on their part. The shuttle driver had walked us through to the lounge for the train and at Cape Town airport, the taxi driver insisted on walking with us to find the car hire stands. Clearly, they thought that this was something they should do, and we were grateful to them for their consideration.

28th January

We had a leisurely walk around the Waterfront this morning, bought a couple of gifts and browsed a few shops and stands. We took a turn on the Ferris wheel which gave us an amazing view of Cape Town, Lions Head, Table Mountain, and a rather hazy Robben Island along with the boats, ships and yachts in and around the harbour and docks. We had lunch outside and under a large umbrella as it was 34 degrees in the shade today.

We then queued for the ferry, looking at some of the museum exhibits as we moved around and noticing the sign which said, 'no guns to be taken to Robben Island'. We enjoyed the ferry journey over to the island, though it would have been good to have been outside and taken in the sea breeze. There was an interesting video about the island and the prison; for which, some of the previous inmates had helped to give a brief history, ensuring we were prepared for our tour on arrival.

The tour of the island was interesting, though extremely sobering. The pain and anguish that one human being can inflict on another is inhumane and all under the conviction of what is seen to be right. We were shown around the prison by a gentleman who had been a political prisoner there himself for seven years, following detention of six months. He said that he would rather do seven years in prison than do that six months in detention again; during which time he had been interrogated and tortured. Many people have ended up with both psychological and physical problems, some died as a direct result of the torture, some took their own lives whilst in detention. Our guide had considered suicide, due to the physical, emotional, and psychological torture that he had suffered. Following his release, his father had said to him, that given some episodes of the torture he had endured it was a wonder that he had managed to father a son. He did not want to discuss the extremes of torture that he had endured, this however gave us some indication of the type of treatment received.

We saw Nelson Mandela's solitary cell, up until 1979 prisoners in those cells slept on concrete, simply a rush mat and a wash bowl. The prisoners worked in the lime quarry on the island, initially this was to be for six months, hard labour. However, it continued for thirteen and a half years for some.

There was a cave in which the prisoners could eat their lunch; there was also a bucket for their toilet. It was agreed amongst the group that they would not use a toilet all day as they did not want to eat in the same space; they agreed to remove the bucket and wait until the end of their eight hour shifts to use a toilet.

There was a pile of stones at the entrance to the quarry now, which Nelson Mandela started on a visit following his release from prison. All the people with him added a stone and it has become quite a pile, a monument to the work that they did there, and the suffering endured. They were given no safety equipment and many people suffered from eye problems and injuries along with many who contracted cancer from the lime dust that they were constantly inhaling, amongst other related illnesses.

We visited the prison dormitories which had been shared by eighteen to twenty inmates with one bucket behind a screen. We were told of some of the deaths that occurred due to torture, and deaths which occurred following torture of so many young men who had been brave enough to stand up for their beliefs and politics.

On our return from Robben Island, we both felt quite drained and emotionally exhausted. Partly perhaps because we had visited the Apartheid museum in Johannesburg, also Soweto and the visit to the prison consolidated what we had thought, experienced, and learned. There was so much information, horror and atrocities to digest.

On our return to the house, we jumped in the car and headed off to Camps Bay at the base of Table Mountain, where we sat on the rocky beach, Rosy had a swim to cool down. The temperature was still 34 degrees at seven thirty in the evening. We stayed and watched the sunset which was absolutely stunning and helped to dilute some of the horrors that we had heard about, earlier in the day.

The fires were still burning at Signal Point and we had watched helicopters taking water from the sea and dropping it on the mountain all day, the fires have been burning for four days now. We enjoyed our visit to Cape Town, we saw and learned so much and experienced a variety of emotions during our stay.

I am keen to learn more about the Apartheid times and the politics of this country; our experiences here have ignited a flame for knowledge about everything to do with South Africa. Such a shame that I cannot have those conversations with Tom.

29th January

We left our lovely accommodation, headed to the airport, and returned the hire car. We are flying to King Shaka airport from Cape Town. Whilst awaiting our flight we spent some time at the airport book shop, looking for books about South Africa, the country, and its politics, we have both developed a real interest in what has and to an extent is still happening here. We have collected a long list of potential reading materials.

Our flight was only two hours and we soon landed at King Shaka Airport Durban. We arranged a hire car as we were advised it was safe to drive in the area so long as we kept to the main roads where possible. We drove out to Tinley Manor on the Dolphin Coast to our new Airbnb. The location was stunning and rather wild. The property was very spacious, comfortable and wonderful views, incredibly wild and rough seas. There was a small beach store next to where we were staying, it did not feel very inviting and until we were inside it was unclear what was on sale. A small group of youths were sitting on a table outside talking about football, they seemed surprised to see us. We went inside to see a man behind a metal grill and counter, he smiled, not a great stock, so it was baked beans on toast for tea tonight. I finished reading my book whilst keeping an eye on the raging sea. Two ibis birds flew passed the window fighting against the wind, being buffeted on their way.

This was a typical seaside area which seemed very quiet at the moment despite it being mid-summer. Children were still in school and like at home I assumed the peak times were in school holidays. However, as the sun disappeared into the sea, various lights appeared, twinkling against the night sky along with many stars. We hoped that the next day would dawn calm and sunny and we may be able to take a walk down to the beach, it looked rather inviting with the Indian Ocean lapping over the sands.

30th January

Much as our accommodation was spacious and had stunning views there was very little to do, apart from perhaps a walk on the beach where the rough sea bombards the rocks and the shore, turning pebbles on its way. So, we took off in the car to St Lucia, a couple of hours up the coast. We drove through interesting landscape of sugar beet, forestry along with the rondavels (round houses) preferred by the Zulu people. Their homesteads were fairly spaced out with collections of a few cows, goats, and chickens around the houses to feed their families.

We passed beef cattle grazing on the side of the main roads with nothing to stop them sauntering across in front of fast-moving traffic. Sheep, goats, and chickens were in pens on the side of the road, for sale, a pop-up market. At various points along the road there were stalls set up as we have seen before, this time selling pineapples, mangoes, plums and marula fruit. Beside the toll booths there was razor wire and concrete bollards to stop the traders coming too close to the oncoming traffic and preventing people parking and causing chaos! As we had seen all over South Africa, people walk for miles and miles to get where they need to be, to work, children to school, and perhaps to visit family, walking along the central reservation and the side of the roads.

As we approached St Lucia, we stopped at a tourist information centre with the intention of asking about boat trips for the day. It turned out to be a craft centre, both local and bought in crafts. It was packed with carved animals, basket ware, jewellery, hats, wooden bowls, and dishes amongst many other beautiful and colourful items. Some of the items were clearly mass produced though some seemed local and hand crafted. There were also items outside to look at, which is where I found the gifts that I wanted for my grandchildren. I was assured by the young man there that he had indeed crafted the hippos and rhinos, the wart hog he said someone else was responsible for, though I was not convinced as he did not know how the different colours had been applied. We had a good look around and as we were about to leave; we found the loo out the back of the building, and we saw a boat on the river, up until then we did not know we were so close to the river. A lady was selling tickets and asked if we wanted to go on a boat trip to see the hippos, crocodiles, and birds. Perfect, no need to go hunting around the town to find a boat trip or parking.

We bought our tickets and climbed aboard sitting on the top deck with a warm breeze engulfing us. Sunscreen and bite spray applied; we were ready for our adventure up the river. As soon as we boarded, we saw a group of hippos closely circled together near the bank. The slow boat up the river was relaxing and leisurely. We only saw one crocodile on the bank of the river and heard perhaps another two splashes, as they turned in the water. Birds were few and far between today, though we saw a cormorant, swifts dipping and diving over the water and of course weaver birds that had woven their nests attached to reeds hanging over the water. Weaver birds simply use available trees, bushes, or reeds to weave their nests, no real preference.

Hippos however were plentiful, we saw about seven family groups huddled together trying to sleep, standing on the bed of the river, looking as though they were floating. They did not seem perturbed by the boats interrupting their dreams, though none of the few boats, on the river went too close. They made wonderful snorting noises, similar to that of pigs, though louder and more persistent. Apparently, there are about one thousand hippos inhabiting this river, along with about twelve hundred crocodiles. So, we were advised that swimming was not permitted and then told where the lifebelts were should there be a problem, we were also told we were quite safe! I would not fancy our chances with or without lifebelts with the inhabitants in this river.

We really enjoyed seeing the hippos as we had only seen one or two when we were on our safari visit. They were fascinating to watch and quite playful when awake. The way the eyes were just above the waterline and then suddenly their huge heads emerged along with their large bodies and then disappeared again whilst they walked along the river-bed to rise again a little further on, mostly staying in their family groups. The young males play-fighting near the riverbanks, such huge mouths and massive teeth. At night they go up out of the river through the reeds to find food and there were signs on the roads saying to beware of the hippos, they would not be a good animal to meet walking along the road, as they frequently do. They appear in people's gardens and in some areas have been found in swimming pools.

Following our relaxing trip up the Mfolozi River, we drove into St Lucia, a small town surrounded by lodges, hotels, self-catering accommodation, restaurants, and craft shops as well as a colourful fruit and vegetable market. We had lunch at the Barraca café which was certainly very tasty and value for money. A pasta dish with a wonderful very creamy cheese sauce. Feeling much better and having spent a little time people watching; tourists. Like us looking, deciding where to stop and have a drink or a meal, children arriving home from school on the bus, deliveries being made and people just enjoying a warm breezy day, we went in search of a supermarket. We picked up a few bits and pieces, sticking to fresh foods and found a few postcards that I wanted to give to the grandchildren with their gifts, the boys are sorted now as I bought a hippo, a rhino and a wart hog from the tourist centre, where we had seen the hippos in their natural habitat. Just Beth to find a gift for now. We then went up to the fresh fruit and vegetable market and bought a huge ripe papaya for our dessert this evening. Twice the size of anything we would find at home and so ripe, you could smell the juice. There was an amazing array of fruit on display, though most things were in packs of five, too much for us as we are off again tomorrow. There was a craft market behind the food market and we had a good look around, realising again how many of the items are mass produced, not that it detered from the individual item, at home most things are mass produced, though when there is a 'craft market' at home it suggests individual hand-made items. The market building was being re-thatched, and it was interesting watching the men at work with an apparent total lack of regard for any safety regulations.

As we had a two-hour drive back to our accommodation, we decided to call it a day, the light was already changing, and it was time to leave. We would like to have seen the hippos coming through the rushes and walking up the road, though would have had to stay until dark for that, we had difficulty finding our accommodation last night and so decided daylight was best. The hippos stay on land all night munching away and we noticed several more signs saying to beware of both hippos and crocodiles near the rivers and to be careful that you did not become their food as we drove away!

The drive home took slightly longer as people were on their way home from their busy working days. There was a lot of road work happening, we saw hundreds of bags of concrete laid out on top of the base layer for a new road, followed by someone walking along tipping the contents out. It seemed that it was then damped down, raked and left to dry off overnight, using the night air to prevent cracking. No sign of any cement mixer lorries here, very much manual work apart from the large earth moving vehicles and rollers, it was interesting to see, how the base layer was constructed.

We enjoyed a relaxed evening and our tea, the papaya was so tasty and fresh, delicious.

31st January

This morning we set off to Shakaland, still in Kwa Zulu Natal, a beautiful drive through the mountains, the Eshowe hills and the Nkwalini Valley to a place overlooking the Umhlatusi River, the birthplace of King Shaka. The scenery was lush and green, sugar beet crops along with forestry and citrus groves flourishing in this amazing climate. Kwa Zulu Natal is bordered by Mozambique, Swaziland, and Lesotho along with other areas of South Africa. It was very picturesque with the Drakensburg Mountains acting as its border with Lesotho. It is an area steeped in history, the Zulus are fiercely proud of their culture and keep it alive here at the largest kraal, 'Shakaland'.

We arrived a little early, hoping that we would be able to take a look around whilst waiting for our room to be prepared, unfortunately this was not allowed, having realised that this was home to Zulu families, we realised why you could not just wander about, invading their privacy. We sat in the bar and had a look at the amazing view over the river and checked out the swimming pool, the Jack fruit growing on the trees. We looked at the dining room and the amazing artwork freeze around the room and the beautiful ceiling, depicting the life and stories of the Zulu nation.

There were two Zulu ladies sat under the tree with their craft wares laid out around them, making their jewellery, one working with tiny beads and the other making rag chokers, also with minute beads, threading the beads onto strands of cotton and then wrapping them very tightly around the strip of rag to make the choker. It was lovely to see them making their crafts. I asked the ladies if I could take a photograph of them while they worked, I rather wish I had just done it and not asked; it caused a bit of a kafuffle as they re-arranged themselves and their belongings, put on some of their jewellery, did up their cardigans and finally allowed me to take a photo at which point they started to sing. Perhaps this is what visitors expect or perhaps it is the pride of the Zulu people to be at their best when they are photographed.

The bee-hive huts were typically all the colours that Africa portrays, rich red, rust and orange bedding with crisp white linen sheets. The blinds for the small curved windows are rust with patterned borders and the room painted with a frieze above white painted walls. The frieze depicts multi coloured diamond shapes, I wondered if that is linked to the diamond mines, though more likely to the shape of the spear point. The ceiling is an amazing feat of woven reeds around the circular building, and then a thatch as the second coat on the outside of the roof.

Sitting by the pool was restful, listening to the birds, and the water bubbling through the filters. I was not planning on going in the pool, though it was a restful place to sit and ponder. I sat and relaxed for an hour, whilst Rosy had her siesta. I wanted to make the most of this wonderful weather, the views and the atmosphere, watching the lizards running into cracks having taken in the sun on the slabs and hear the birds, singing their solo songs. We have one week left in this beautiful country before we head home to wintery days, so sunscreen on and bring on the sun. A young couple from Argentina joined me by the pool and were encouraging me to add Argentina to my bucket list, they came from Mendoza.

That evening we had a very pleasant few hours being introduced to the Zulu Culture, from the herbalist, to throwing spears and the story of Shaka through film. We experienced the Zulu dances and cultural undertones of the courtship rituals as well as war cries and dance. All ages were involved in the display and all clearly enjoyed themselves. We were then given a very tasty and substantial meal. We had a long chat to one of the waitresses and viewed each other's children in photos on our phones. She told us about her sons, one who was a chef in Durban and the other who was still at college and lived with her here at the kraal. We returned to our hut, having checked our messages whilst we were in the bar with Wi-Fi. We had had a very full day and thoroughly enjoyed the experience. We were to be shown a few more cultural experiences in the morning straight after breakfast before we leave. It had been thirty-five degrees and we were both ready for a read and a good night's sleep.

Tomorrow we depart from King Shaka, Durban airport

for Nelsprit to visit Graskop and the surrounding area, our final adventure on this truly amazing holiday.

1st February

The night was very hot, though the beds and the room comfortable. The lizards were running around up and down the walls and in the woven roof, however they did not bother us once we worked out what the noises were in the roof. We enjoyed a wonderful spread for breakfast to set us up for the day and were then invited to attend the rest of our Zulu experience. We were reminded as to why King Shaka had the spear shortened, the reason being that if you threw the long spear and missed your target, that person could then pick up your spear, throw it back and perhaps kill you. The short spear was used for hand-to-hand fighting, with a much better chance of killing your enemy. We also had the courtship ceremony demonstrated by some of the teenagers which was interesting, and they made it fun. It all took place by the water hole and the girls carrying water pots on their heads and giving of gifts to their chosen one.

We left Shakaland having been given an insight into the Zulu culture, by the people themselves. It was colourful and interesting. I found a pretty Zulu carving of a girl with the beads around her neck, a gift for Beth, just before we left. Whilst the people here consisted of different families, they interact as one big family, they clearly enjoyed singing and dancing and do so whilst carrying out their daily chores. The young man who had been showing us around had brought an apple with him to give to his mum, she was sitting on the ground with two other ladies getting ready to rope new reeds in order to do a roof repair. He shared his concerns that she was too old and should not have to work now, that he should provide for her, but he had chosen to stay at the kraal and did not earn enough for her to retire.

We reached King Shaka airport and returned the hire car, had our luggage wrapped and booked ourselves in for our flight. We arrived at the gate to find that our flight was delayed by one and a quarter-hour, giving me the chance to write my journal. On our drive back to the airport we had seen a grey monkey crossing the road, sadly a little further along we saw one that had met its fate in the road, these were the only none domestic animals we had seen during our drive which was quite unusual. Our flight delay did not cause us any problems and once we arrived, we collected the hire car and made our way to Graskop with a slight detour to see Pilgrim's Rest on the way, worth a visit for another day.

Having arrived at our hostel, we went off to do some supermarket shopping as we do have a fridge available in our room, along with a kettle. We decided picnics were to be the order for this trip as there are so many wonderful sites to see. We were planning on following the 'Panorama Route' to see all of the main sites tomorrow, just in case the weather changes, we had been incredibly lucky so far and don't want to tempt fate. Having bought all our picnic food we went to a restaurant for tea that specialised in South African food, it was delicious.

When we left the restaurant, we realised that we had miscalculated and taken our eye off the ball. It was dark and there were no streetlights. The paving stones where very uneven, cracked and broken in places and so I decided it was safer to walk along the road facing the traffic, there was not much traffic and there were large groups of people on the pavements, so rather than walk through people we stayed on the road, avoiding the darkest spots and groups of people where we could. As we walked down the side street, we realised that the taxi rank was also a place where all the young people hang out, enjoying music and each other's company in the evenings. We were quite pleased to get back and finally inside the security gate, having finally found the keys in one of Rosy's many pockets. Standing outside we did feel a bit vulnerable and silly for not keeping to our safety rules. The area was isolated and very dark and there was a group of youngsters hanging around where we were staying, admittedly on the other side of the lane. No one caused us any concern.

We were not feeling threatened, just a bit vulnerable as we had not checked the lighting, the area and leaving it until dark, with two bags of shopping to carry back, suggesting that we would also have had purses with us!

2nd February

Heavy rain fell, continuing most of the night. We woke to a thick mist obscuring everything in sight and yet still decided to get on our way early having been told by our host that the mist would clear within an hour or so. So much to see and do here in Mpumalanga. It seemed as if we had been rather too optimistic when we left Daan's place, however within an hour the mist had cleared, and we had a beautiful clear sunny day until about 4.30pm when we had a heavy downpour whilst driving over Robbers Pass.

Our first stop of the day was to have been God's Window, however we decided to wait for a clear view and the mist, whilst lifting would have obscured the full view. We continued along the Panorama Route to the Berlin Falls, slightly lower altitude, and a lot less mist. We were the only visitors so early in the morning, and it was beautiful. The stall holders were still setting up with all their wares, some great temptations, though we were not buying today. The birds singing, the flowers bright and the falls rushing in full flow after last night's rain.

Our next two brief stops were Viewpoint of Lowveld and the Three Rondavels, the latter are three mountains shaped like the round houses that the Zulu people live in. Stunning, lush green vegetation against the red rock of the Blyde River Canyon and the sun creating great long shadows over the hills. It is so hard to describe the landscape, you really do have to be there, amazing, breath-taking, stunning, beautiful are words that just don't capture the expanse, the colour, light and the pure magic of Africa.

Our second longer stop was at Bourke's Luck Potholes, this was a definite get out and walk visit as opposed to stand in awe of the breath-taking views. I had been recommended to visit here by a friend and it did not disappoint. As we walked through from the car park we watched as a group of children danced, they were quite young some of them, all dressed up and thoroughly enjoying themselves singing and dancing on a grassy area. The potholes have been formed by grit and stones carried by the rivers Blyde and Treur, carving out these amazing features in the rock over hundreds of years. We stayed and enjoyed the views, the rushing waters, climbing over rocks and boulders, watching lizards, listening to birds singing. I climbed a metal ladder thinking I could walk a bit further up the river and then saw the sign saying strenuous walk, I had enough trouble getting back down the ladder, though I was helped down the last high step that had seemed easy on the way up! At that point I had lost Rosy; she had walked off in a different direction and was sitting contemplating the view. We took photos, enjoyed the flora, fauna, and the sound of rushing waters where the two rivers meet. We had our picnic in the allocated area, and as always enjoyed people watching, sitting under the shade of a big old tree. Before we left, we had a look around the souvenir stands, as always so many beautiful things, not enough space in the suitcase, though I did buy a wooden map of South Africa, only a small one, I have seen them several times, beautifully carved, and finally found the right size for what I wanted. As my children instigated this adventure and paid for my plane ticket, I wanted a small map to hang near the family group photo that they gave me for my 60th birthday, I am so grateful to them, I would never have done this if it had not for them.

The Echo Caves were just outside Ohrigstad and were the last stop of the day for us. It was one of those drives along unmade roads when you wonder if you will ever find the place. Our guide, when we finally arrived at the caves told us that the caves were found by accident when a farmer had lost his cattle back in the 1920s and a detailed search took place to find them. The cattle had somehow found an entrance to the hidden caves. The farmer decided that they were so interesting that they should be opened to the public, they have now been declared an historical monument. These caves are said to be amongst the oldest in the world, they stretch for about 40km though the tour does not go more than about 2 km. I am not sure what I expected to find when I booked our tour around the caves. I had not thought about the physical exertion at all. The caves were fascinating, limestone stalactites and stalagmites, squeezing through narrow gaps and on my hands and knees through low openings. They were called Echo caves as there is a dolomite rock that emits an echo for miles if hit with a hard object deep inside the cave. For the people who lived in those caves it was a warning that could be heard far and wide if there were other tribes on the rampage, or other threats to the people. It was certainly very loud and echoed.

We were told that these were limestone and dolomite

caves, up to about one hundred and fifty people had lived there and various items were found in the caves, many of the exhibits can be seen in the 'Museum of Man' which you pass on the way up the unmade road to the caves. There were remains of people buried in the caves, earthenware pots, cooking utensils along with early pestle and mortars were also found. It was a fascinating visit, though having hopped around at the Bourke's potholes this morning, I admit that I was quite exhausted, the ninety-eight steps to climb out of the caves was quite a feat for me to complete. The other people on the tour were much younger and it seemed fitter, than me! We were ready for a drink in the café by the time we got our breath back.

We drove back via Robbers Pass to view more amazing scenery and despite a heavy downpour, we were not disappointed. We saw three klipspringer antelope and a grey fox, Rosy saw a baboon climbing a rock face and then I saw a couple of grey monkeys perched one each end of a roof in Pilgrims Rest, initially I thought they were chimney pots.

Pilgrims Rest dates back to 1873, a heritage site from back in the goldrush days, it had beautifully restored original properties, built in most cases of corrugated iron with striking red corrugated rooves. We stopped to take photos today just in case the weather is inclement tomorrow.

A wonderful day of fabulous scenery, amazing sights, including a turquoise lizard with a red tail. Africa really is a world in one country. We had driven through a part of

Limpopo when on our way to the caves today. There had been an outbreak of foot and mouth in Limpopo, announced on the radio, we were very careful to scrub our shoes with disinfectant before visiting anywhere else.

Come evening we snacked on food that we had left over from our shopping and were really too tired to do anything else. What a fantastic day of both physical and emotional awe and wonder.

3rd February

It was very foggy this morning so we set off at about 10.00am and drove down to Sabie and then off to the Horseshoe Falls. We drove through a busy and industrious timber area with huge timber yards, massive lorries stacked high with logs. The roads had loads of pot-holes, the size of craters and then we found ourselves on a red dirt track with logs scattered across the road where they had become dislodged from trucks, boulders and pot-holes the size of craters in the roads. Rosy was driving an obstacle course, and we thought yesterday was extreme! A cartoon came to mind, Rosy and me in the tincan hire car having fallen in the crater, swallowed whole and us peeping up over the edge to see what was happening around us.

We finally arrived at the Horse-shoe Falls and were surprised to see holiday accommodation available at the site and at the end of a 4.5km dirt road. We saw the same yesterday at Echo Caves. Entrepreneurial people.

The climb up to the falls was very steep, uneven high steps, slippery from last night's rain. It was worth the climb to see the falls, two shafts of water torrenting down the steep drop. Rosy climbed a little further than me as since yesterday my hip had been playing up and I really did not want to take a fall all the way out here, in the middle of nowhere the day before we were due to fly home, not sure that I would want to carry Rosy either should she take a tumble!

We were engulfed in flora and fauna, different from some of what we had already seen, it was almost rain-forest vegetation, damp and humid. Amazing butterflies, including the large yellow, black, and white with its swallow tail flitting around. They never stayed still long enough to get a picture of them, beautiful to watch though.

On our steady and precarious descent from the falls we met a South African couple with their little boy, about four or five years old. By the time we got down to the car park area, they were over by the river's edge and excitedly announced that they had seen a green snake, a green mambo, very venomous, the fellow suggested, though according to our google search that would have been unlikely in that area. The snake however had a frog in its mouth, and no, we did not go close enough to see it. Apart from a puff adder on safari we had managed to avoid seeing any snakes so far. It seemed strange to me that this couple had left their child, admittedly outside of a taped off area, with no shoes on, whilst they went in, with flipflops on their feet to investigate further. They were circling the snake to make it show itself, the African man who looked after the car park was saying 'Baas' and gesticulating that they should leave it alone. They ignored him, he then made a point of standing near the boy, perhaps to make sure he was safe, he was after all standing barefoot in long grass. I doubt that a snake would take note of a taped off area! The lady who was selling her wares, turned, looking rather annoyed and walked away, back to her stall having come to see what all the noise was about.

Rosy and I were stood well back and did not see the possibly venomous snake that was being goaded by this couple. It eventually slipped into the river they said, I imagine it would not have got any peace otherwise.

Having run the gauntlet back down the red dirt track we headed for Long Tom Pass on a somewhat better road. Another recommendation from a friend. The Pass had the backdrop of the Drakensburg Mountains. We thought that the Blyde River Canyon was remarkable, yesterday. The immense scale of the mountains viewed from the Pass was simply awe-inspiring. Every direction that you looked the views were tremendous, we were certainly overwhelmed by it all. We stopped at Devils Knuckles where the last position of the Long Tom Canon in action, was displayed, and had our picnic. The highest point is 2150m above sea level. It was like sitting on the top of Africa, an Africa that I had never imagined existed. They say it gets under your skin; it certainly did for me as it obviously had for Tom.

The mist came and went as we drove through, and on top of the Pass, leaving us in a mystical world of wonder and extremes, as we looked around us. We bought a few gifts from the lone lady selling her wares at the site of the canon, a string of beads for Elaine and a bracelet for Rosy's daughter. It was good to see the lady making these gifts herself.

We encountered enormous trucks transporting coal up and down the Pass, apparently since the last election the transport system has all but broken down, trains no longer run, and the trucks cause massive potholes in the roads. More accidents are happening. Perhaps our train to Cape Town was also affected by those same issues.

We continued along towards Lyndenburg, situated at the end of the Pass. We made several stops to take photos and to take in the views, the camera whilst giving you the prompts and memories cannot possibly capture more than the essence of the beauty that was before us; nor the enormity of the mountains, hills, depth of gulley's, rivers and the pure space that surrounded us, and to make her day Rosy saw a marico sunbird.

We saw a lone Springbok on the Pass. From there we drove back through Sabie to Graskop and then to God's Window. We passed baboons and monkeys on both sides of the road, the baboon troupe, about thirty of them were enjoying the forestry area. The monkeys were staying on their side of the road away from the baboons, about a dozen monkeys. God had his window open for us today, and oh my, what a view. Once again it had been a day for wonderous views that made us feel like miniatures against the vastness and scale. The views were spectacular. There were monkeys to greet and amuse us by playing in the trees with a minute baby tagging along. For the first time since Cape Town, we found ourselves surrounded by a bus full of European visitors and noticed just how noisy groups of people can become.

From God's Window we moved on to Wonder View, no monkeys there, collared ravens instead, with their large parrot like black beaks. The views lived up to our expectation again today, we then visited The Pinnacle; a great pillar erupting from the forest floor. We saw more daasies, a South African striped mouse, very striking stripes down its back, and a tinkerbird.

Once again, we had enjoyed a sensational day, full of surprises and wonder at everything this country has to offer. We celebrated our day at Wagner's where we ate the night we arrived, this time we had the car, so no need to walk back in the dark. The food was excellent, tasty, and African.

We caught up with messages home and a few photos to show the family what we had been up to. Feeling quite exhausted now and ready for a good night's sleep. I cannot believe that we only have one day left to explore this beautiful and diverse country before flying back to Johannesburg and then home.

4th February

Panorama Gorge Falls Graskop, our last day of exploring before starting the homeward journey tomorrow. The weather was sunny and no fog this morning despite the warnings of torrential rain all day. We set off to the Graskop Lift to go down to the floor of the gorge, to explore the trees, birds, animals and insects which live alongside the falls. The lift travels down fifty metres to where there are wooden walkways and suspension bridges over the water. As we entered, we went under a beautifully crafted stained-glass hanging which portrayed some of the wildlife, fauna, and flora that we might see.

The six hundred metres of walking a circular route including several sets of steps. It was beautifully crafted, and you felt as if you have stepped into another world. We saw some insects and a few birds, though not many, perhaps we were too far down to see the birds, though we did see a couple of ground birds. Birdsong was evident, though seemed to be higher up towards the canopy, we saw rock martins darting about, high up in the gorge.

The butterflies were quite beautiful and one that we saw was as large as my hand the Queen Alexandra's Birdwing, yellow and brown with a little orange on the body; they danced between the trees and in and out of the boulders by the water. They never stayed still long enough to see clearly, so large that initially I thought they were small birds darting about. As we walked along there were useful boards so that we could identify what we saw and helped us to look out for certain things, many of the trees were labelled and the walkways were all sculptured around the existing growth in the gorge.

We heard Cicadas which omitted a noise like an alarm,

piercing, continuous with little or no change of pitch. Initially I thought it was the alarm on the lift. We noticed a little black beetle with a small red spot on its back and a couple of black, cricket like creatures which were running happily along the wooden rails.

The water tumbled seventy metres down into the gorge over natural slate steps into a pool and then rushed on its way through the gorge over boulders and rocks. We visited the gorge twice as the entry fee allowed unlimited access throughout the day and we hoped that by visiting each end of the day we might see more wildlife. Just as well really as I mislaid my sunglasses during our first visit and managed to collect them on afternoon visit. As we left the Graskop lift we were caught in a rain storm of stair-rods and of course no coats to hand, so had to make a run for it back to the car.

Between our two visits to Graskop lift, we spent a couple of hours at Pilgrim's Rest, visiting the hotel which was still open to guests and beautifully decorated in 1930s Art Deco style. The old post office with its switchboard and notices along with the museum with all the minerals that had been found in the area, was fascinating. And of course, the stories of gold mining which gave rise to the settlers who found sufficient gold here to make it worth staying, having tried many other locations before-hand. Hence the name Pilgrim's Rest, time to settle and reap the rewards of the gold deposits.

On our return to Graskop we had a look around some of the local shops which we had noticed when driving around.

We bought gifts to bring home and watched a lady set up outside a shop with a loom, making beautiful silken scarves, I bought one for a gift. We returned to Daan's Place to make ready for our departure in the morning.

We finished our day with a spectacular thunder and lightning storm, just as we had started on our first night in Johanessburg four weeks ago. That is the magic of Africa!

5th February

Leaving Graskop in the morning felt quite surreal. As if those four weeks had never happened. We had used every minute of our time and immersed ourselves in the culture and landscape of this fabulous country. The people had been friendly and helpful.

Yes, we have had a couple of moments feeling a little uncomfortable, rather than vulnerable or unsafe. One of those times was waiting outside Woolworth's supermarket in Norwood Johanessburg for the uber to arrive, feeling that all eyes were on us. We were the only white people on the street. Another situation in Norwood was interesting when we went to a café for a cup of tea, being ushered to a corner right at the back of the café, even though it was empty and there was plenty of seating outside. Was that because we were white?

For me, driving over the mountains in the mist and fog with no people or other cars in sight made us vulnerable. The fog was thick in parts and heavy rain falling; being aware of the number of car-jackings, I felt a little uncomfortable. And lastly when we left it until after dark to walk back from the restaurant to Daan's Place. I suppose a thought did enter my head when I saw the 'car-jacking hotspot' sign as we drove from Johanessburg out to Hartbeespoort Dam! However, we had followed advice, kept our wits about us and stayed safe; without taking anything away from any pleasure during our fantastic adventure in South Africa.

I felt as if I had grown, with the knowledge that I had gained here. I certainly felt that I understood Tom better, and could understand why he chose South Africa to call his home for his last twenty-five years.

We flew from Kruger Mpumalanga International (KMI) Airport to Johannesburg, though we initially found ourselves at the private Nelsprit airport and had to retrace our tracks. Thankfully, we had left plenty of time to get to the airport. On arrival we were met by a herd of Springbok, which was a lovely surprise and a fitting farewell. We had seen mongoose and monkeys as we drove, and so finished our travels still enjoying the wildlife.

At the airport we bought our last few gifts and when we reached Johannesburg we went to check in, we had a very frustrating one and a half-hour wait at check-in, having been told it would be 4pm, we continued to wait until 4.30pm and then 5pm. Eventually we checked in the luggage, still wrapped from KMI. We quickly went off to find the Spur Steakhouse and met Brenda and her husband John. We returned the phone and the charger which had kindly been loaned to us for the duration. We had a leisurely meal with them, regaling them with our adventures. Brenda was telling us about her efforts with the Home Affairs Office to obtain Tom's death notice, which had after two and a half years eventually come to light. Brenda is soon to move home to the UK and was telling us of her plans. We said our goodbyes and set off at a pace to departures, stopping to buy a couple of books on the way.

Our flight took off at 20.35. We saw the sunrise as we approached Doha and a spectacular orange sun blended with small puffy clouds of gold, filled the sky as we landed. A quick changeover with ample exercise to loosen up our old limbs following the first flight was helpful.

I felt very emotional when we took off from Johanessburg as if I were leaving something behind, and I was, Tom. For the first time ever, I felt like I was not ready to go home yet, such mixed emotions, so hard to put into words.

I kept thinking about the amazing four weeks we had enjoyed and about the country itself. A country so rich in minerals, steeped in history, with a people so strong and proud of their cultural traditions. Young people had said to us, how is our country so rich and yet we are so poor? The political undertones are causing a widespread unrest with an election on its way. The transport infrastructure/system has suffered greatly under the present government, trains are few and far between. Roads are, in parts, badly pot-holed by the enormous trucks carrying minerals, logs and coal by road rather than rail. The trains that are still running appear to require a good overhaul and maintenance.

The corruption that we had been told about shows where the country's wealth is being syphoned. The gap between rich and poor is getting wider daily. Poverty is visible in certain areas, people who have nothing, some not even a cardboard box to sleep on and all, in spite of a system that allocates free housing to people out of work – though the waiting time can be up to about fifteen years and then if you should find a job within that time, you may lose out on the house. We had been told that in some cases where housing had been allocated, officials could come along and sell the property evicting the tenants. Imagine how that would feel for people who had waited for up to fifteen years to live their dream, a home of their own.

Despite the history of the British in Africa, we had felt no resentment from individuals, if anything quite the opposite. Particularly, though not only the young people, seemed excited that we were from the United Kingdom and were interested in our country and how things work. It was a little worrying that particularly the young people seemed to think that London is still paved with gold. In so many ways South Africa is a far richer country especially in relation to gold and other minerals.

It will be interesting to follow the news and politics of South Africa now that we have visited and experienced the country through travelling around and learning more about it during our adventures. I am interested in what we have been told and what we have observed first-hand. I know little about politics and yet feel that I know just a little more now, about what the people feel in this country, both black and white. I hope that the government listens to the people and that they continue to create a great future for the country that they love.

Our flight was quite smooth, flying over desert and snow-capped mountains. It was so bright as the snow became more widespread. We flew over the lakes at Van near Tabriz. Spookily the sky goes a dark blue with blue lakes and fluorescent white snow. All to do with the lighting inside and outside of the plane I suppose. The sky was getting black now and the cabin had become dark. Our side of the plane looked like night and yet the other side was still light and bright. We were flying towards Erzurum and Ankara, perhaps over the Black Sea and now flying over Constanta. We land at Gatwick at 12.35 on the 6th February.

As it became too dark to see outside, I decided to have a sleep, everyone else seemed to have settled down with their eye masks and blankets. I had not really slept since we boarded the plane at 20.15 yesterday evening and with the time zones, I was all out of kilter. And then, the turbulence began!

What an amazing adventure, so many memories and experiences to hold in my heart. Africa has certainly got under my skin and Tom has become more real in my mind.

We arrived at Gatwick safely and on time, everything moved fairly fast and we were outside ringing Rosy's partner to tell him where we were, within minutes we had loaded our luggage and were speeding our way home to Cornwall.

I was not sure of the emotions were that were swimming around my head. I was looking forward to getting home and seeing the family and of course Bertie my dog. And yet I felt sad that our journey was over. It took nearly a year to finalise all the planning and somehow four weeks had flown passed, I could have stayed happily for another few weeks.

Africa gets under your skin, yes it does, it did for Tom and I agree whole heartedly with that sentiment. It is a country that changes around every corner. It is full of colour, light and sound. The people are friendly, welcoming, and interesting. The birds, animals, flora and fauna are colourful and beautiful, as are the people. The history and culture whilst sad, barbaric and terrifying, showing the worst in human behaviours, is what makes this country what it is today. We have, I have had, the time of my life, an adventure that cannot be replicated. I have seen so much. I have opened my eyes and learned so much, things that I can never unlearn or un-see.

There is so much of Africa still to see, I may just have to go back and see some more!

Since returning from South Africa, I have heard from Brenda, who has been relentless in finding information about Tom for me. Bitter-sweet information, I now have his

Unabridged Death Certificate. It states that he had been ill for four years and six months, he had multiple myeloma and died from cardiac arrest whilst in hospital in Johannesburg. Tom died 13th January 1979. It seems he was alone, as it was an official who reported the death and organised the cremation. Auntie Bet always told me that his wife, Isabella was upset that Tom had been cremated and it seemed that she was not in the country when he died. I believe they had a volatile relationship and he was alone at this time. He died age sixty-one years, so young. For his wife, who has dementia now, her memories are of a happy life in South Africa and a loving, happy marriage. What a wonderful thing the mind is, I am so pleased that her memories are of happy days, with the man who was her 'everything'.

Thanks to Brenda, I now know where Tom was cremated, though I am still trying to find out where his ashes were spread.

Chapter 10

Wales and the North West

It has taken me a couple of months to settle back to being at home, it is strange how travel can affect people differently. I think that both Rosy and I have found it difficult to revert to our regular routines and duties. It is March now and Ian and I are heading off to visit Aggie and family up north, and whilst on route we will be visiting Wales, my mother's family home in Colwyn Bay, Rhuddlan church and cemetery to see if we can find my great, great grand-father and great, great grand-mother's resting place.

I have just had a long conversation with Edna on the telephone and once again some questions are answered and raised. We chatted about our impending trip and about Edna's busy social events including the choir and hand bells. Once again Edna was saying how close Tom, Pat as she knew him, and my mother had seemed to be and then suddenly it was over, no explanations given.

My mother's father, my grandfather was a policeman, so was in a reserved occupation and so did not go to war. Once he had retired from the police, he became a security guard. He was part of the Plymouth Brethren Group, perhaps that was an issue with Tom being Roman Catholic, though I doubt that would have made too much difference, except that my mother was absolutely clear that I was to be brought up Church of England or Non-Conformist, yet Edna tells me that she herself refused to be confirmed in the Church of England.

Edna remembers spending happy weeks during the summer holidays at Colwyn Bay, her father was a teacher. My mother was born in Colwyn Bay, and after she was three years of age, she lived with her parents and grandparents at Avon Terrace. My grandmother was quite poorly at this stage with MS and so Margaret, my mother's aunt spent many an hour caring for and entertaining my mother. When my mother's aunt married, they stayed close and when Edna was born my mother was nine years of age and so Edna and my mother spent many happy summers together, like sisters. They remained very close for the rest of my mother's life. I was looking forward to visiting Wales and the places that Edna has such fond memories of spending time with my mother and their grand-parents.

My great, great grand-father Thomas Davies was a coachman, having started out as a groom and probably a stable boy before that. At the time he married Margaret

Jefferys, he was working at Bodrhyddan Hall, which belonged to, and still belongs to Lord Langford's family. I contacted the Hall to see if they had records of their staff, sadly because of a fire years ago, there are no longer any records to see. The fire was caused by a land agent who had been 'cooking the books' it seems. The fire was to cover up evidence of his wrong doings. So, whilst I have not managed to further my family tree, I have been told that the Hall is open to the public for a few days a week from June until September. Our next visit will include a detour to the Hall to see the stables where my great, great grandfather worked, and you never know there may be some photographs somewhere of the carriages and horses that he looked after. Perhaps my love of horses and riding is the result of both nature and nurture.

For Matt's birthday, one of my grandsons, I organised a 'driving' experience. At eight years of age, he was driving a carriage of two beautiful Gelderland horses. Matt also rides and has a great affinity with horses. He drove so well that he is hoping to go and help at the stables during the summer holidays.

We set off north later than hoped, though still left home by 9.00am along with Bertie, my dog. The weather was good for driving, clear skies, no rain, a definite chill in the air. I had checked the oil and filled the washers before leaving home.

It seemed a long drive, having stopped every couple of hours to stretch our legs and for Bertie to have a walk around,

Ian with a bad knee and me with bad hips make a great pair. Ageing is no fun! As we came off the M6 we found ourselves in beautiful green countryside, driving through pretty villages, with many red brick Victorian style houses, several lodge houses belonging to the larger estates of a similar vintage. There were a few thatched cottages scattered along the way. Chimneys that seemed out of proportion with the houses, beautiful designs, mostly Victorian I expect, though some may have been earlier.

We arrived at Rhuddlan just before 4pm. The light was still good. We saw the church on our left as we came over the river. A pretty little fifteenth century church. We drove around and parked, spending about forty-five minutes checking every gravestone as I had received confirmation that both great, great grandparents were buried here. It was interesting looking at the gravestones through the ages. Davies is clearly a very common name in Wales, as is Williams and Jones. Sadly, we did not find the Davies that we had hoped to find. Having searched to no avail we decided that where there were some stones placed back against the wall, purple slate, that the inscriptions must have worn off over the years. Over one hundred and twenty years is a long time.

We drove up into the village, we could quite easily have walked, though we did not know how far we needed to go. Number 5 High Street where my great, great grandmother had lived until her death and is now a cheese shop, with a flat above. My great grandmother had also lived on this road at number 10. We did not know that at the time, so that will be another visit for the future.

Our next visit was to Colwyn Bay to find the house where my great grandparents had lived. Where Edna and my mother spent many happy summer holidays. The house must have

been quite full with my great grand-parents, grand-parents and Edna's mum and dad, Edna and my mother all staying together. Happy times as Edna remembers.

As we left Colwyn Bay, we passed what seemed to be a large slate quarry with a truck bridge across the road so that the quarry slate could be loaded straight onto cargo vessels, not sure if this is still in operation now. We also saw several castles of different styles and age, rolling hills

My maternal great grand-parents Sarah Matilda and George Davies outside Avon Terrace

and farmland to our right. We left with enough light to see the sea on our left sweeping around towards the mouth of the Mersey before arriving at our Travel Lodge for the night.

We will definitely be returning to Wales for a longer visit when we next head up to Merseyside in September. So much to see and information to search out. On this trip we did not have time to visit the church and graveyard where my great grandparents are resting, along with my grandmother.

Whilst visiting Merseyside we made good use of our National Trust membership, visiting Rufford Hall. Bertie, my dog enjoyed his runs in Carleen Wood, and we visited Aggie and auntie Marg, taking her to visit Quarry Bank Mill for the day. We organised the trolleybus to take us around the site which was quite steep. The Styll Village was fascinating, it was built to accommodate the workforce to ensure that no one was ever late for work.

Apart from one, the houses still have long term tenants though no longer Mill workers. One of the houses No. 13 is a listed building and protected under conservation law. It shows a wonderful history of how the properties were originally used. The history of the people who lived there and the way in which the house was shared, with extended family and lodgers at different times was interesting. The rents were reasonable, and the workers had spare money to buy meat, bread, and extras from the village shop. All the houses had allotments and small garden space. The school is still in use and now has one hundred and eighteen pupils of primary age. I have noticed on records for my mother's family that many people took in lodgers at this time.

On our way to visit Edna at Stockport we stopped off at Dunham Massey, another National Trust property; a wonderful space for Bertie to let off steam and have a good walk as we were to do a lot of driving today to take us back down to Bristol for the night before our onward journey home tomorrow. Once again we arrived at Edna's at midday and Ian took Bertie and headed off to the pub whilst Edna and I had a look at some more photos that she had found and a good chat. We met up with Ian an hour and a half later, he had been walking around with Bertie as he was not sure whether he could take a dog into the pub.

Once again, the pub produced a good meal and we enjoyed a catch up. We took Edna home and checked that everything was in place for her flight down to visit us in May. We left at about three thirty and arrived at Bristol eight thirty in the evening. We have had a good day and it was lovely to spend time with Edna; once again I have a little more insight regarding my mother, to add to my story.

On leaving Bristol we turned off to visit Tyntesfield, a Victorian Gothic House that felt family orientated and friendly, belonging to the National Trust. Beautiful wood panelling and wonderful carvings. The volunteers were deeply knowledgeable, they really wanted to share what they knew about the family and the house, pointing out small and significant secrets. We spent about three hours at the house, having walked Bertie first of course and left him with food and water in the car. It was a damp and drizzly day so with the windows just cracked open he was wonderfully comfortable. We will keep the gardens for another day, given the weather and the time, as we needed to head home. What an enjoyable time we have had visiting family and joining more dots up in my family history.

I am so looking forward to Edna coming to stay and I have already got an idea of places that I shall take her to visit. Apparently, my mother and Edna visited Perranporth on holiday sometimes, and that is a place she would like to revisit. I am pleased that my mother came to Cornwall as well as Devon, it has such a special place in my heart. We will also be visiting the crematorium at Exeter. My mother's birthday will be in June and so Edna and I will take some flowers as an early gift. I will be going up again on her birthday and will be able to refresh them then.

Edna in Cornwall

Edna came to stay towards the end of May, she flew from Manchester to Newquay and I picked her up, bringing her home via our lovely coast road, we stopped halfway home to eat a sandwich with a view of the sea. Edna stayed for just five nights as she was worried that she may outstay her welcome! We had a wonderful time, the weather was not hot, but mostly warm and dry.

Edna accompanied me to the Lead Mines where I often walk the dogs and she clearly has a liking for dogs, and them, for her, as my mother had. We visited Wadebridge having had a drive through Pencarrow Gardens, the Rhododendrons were in full bloom and very colourful. Ian and Edna walked up through the town and watched some filming that was taking place and then sat and had an ice cream whilst John and I had a meeting to attend. The next morning, I had a changeover at Waves End once that was done, suggested to Edna that we took the ferry to Padstow and had a coffee before returning home for lunch. Edna took the wind out of my sails when we arrived in Padstow, by suggesting that we went out on the Jubilee Queen, which takes you for a one-and-a-half-hour cruise around the coast. We found a coffee shop and then walked over to the boat. I was a little worried about Edna walking down the harbour steps, to board the boat, though with the help of the boatmen she managed perfectly. She is an incredibly determined, independent and gutsy lady. We had a wonderful day and talked a lot. The beauty of Edna coming to stay is that we have got to know each other quite well and the conversations have been natural and unrushed, frequently with more information about my mother and the family.

During her visit Edna has finally met all the family, had afternoon tea with Clare, spent time at the cider farm, lunch with Elaine, Dave and Freddie, my youngest grandson; and enjoyed a lovely family roast meal at Philip and Lucy's, meeting Beth, Dan and Matt and so has now met all my children, my son in law and daughter in law, as well as all the grandchildren and my sister Clare, Jo was not home at the time, so perhaps next time. Suddenly her family has become big, when she thought that she was the last living member. Edna had always known of my existence, and whilst she felt that she would receive a letter from me one day, she could not possibly have known when. It was a wonderful occasion for our family to meet each other, and for Edna, this must have all been a big surprise, as well as hopefully a good one. Edna also met John, on several brief occasions as he flew in and out of the house, home or off to work. He thought she was pretty 'cool.'

We have visited Perranporth where both Edna and my mother holidayed on occasions, along with many other destinations, both here and abroad. And of course, we went to visit my mother at the crematorium in Exeter and took her some flowers, well actually it was a pot of bright yellow chrysanthemums. We found a seat and sat and chatted about my mother and my father; discussing what had happened between them, surmising rather, as we will never know the full story. We talked about my mother's short though happy marriage to Frank and later we drove out to the farmhouse where they had lived. It was quite surreal to be sitting in the sun, at the crematorium discussing people that I have never known and yet are such a huge part of me.

Our day had not started well, as my car developed some problems and at Sourton Down we spent two hours waiting for the RAC to kindly come out and fix the problem. My biggest concern was that we would manage to get to the crematorium before it closed, as Edna was due to fly home the next day. We had to forego our lunch at a nice pub that I had booked for today, as they stopped serving at 2pm. Ian cancelled our table. Instead, it was sandwiches, crisps and a bottle of drink from the garage. Edna wanted to see the place where my mother's ashes had been spread and I wanted to be with Edna and my mother. That may seem strange those of you who are reading this, but it was especially important to me.

During her stay Edna called me 'Margaret', my mother's name, on several occasions, and more as her stay continued. At first, I was a little worried that Edna may become confused when she went home, realising that Margaret, my mother had died nearly five years ago. However, she said that I was so like my mother in looks, some characteristics and mannerisms; she could not help herself. It was comforting in many ways to be called Margaret, especially as I quickly realised that Edna was ok, not confused in any way. Edna's visit has helped me once again to come to know more about my mother which is what I have wanted, and needed to know, all my life. I like the fact that I am so like her, I also like the fact that I have many of my father's characteristics too. I feel so lucky to have found Edna after all these years. For so long I thought that I would never know anything about my mother, and now, less than a year since first contact with Edna I feel that I know my mother quite well. And then, comes the 'if only', once again.

We cannot change the past; we can only plan for the future and live for the day. I hope that Edna will come for another visit and maybe stay a little longer if she would like. We will be visiting her on our next trip up north. We are also visiting Wales again, next June and we will definitely include Bodrhyddan Hall where my great, great, grandfather was a coachman so many years ago. I have been trying again through Ancestry to find more information about his family. That is proving difficult, though I am finding some leads, so fingers crossed for a break-through soon. Edna is convinced that there is a family secret, or scandal to be found. So, we will keep going, at some point things will click into place. The difficulty is that not all the records are accurate and so I have a span of three potential years when my great, great grandfather was born. I am going through all the dates with Ancestry in the hope of finding the right one, it is not easy. All I seem to have found so far is that he was about twenty years senior to my great, great, grandmother and perhaps that was a secret, a scandal.

Chapter 11
St Olaves Home for 'Fallen Girls'

Since I first found out about St Olaves, where I was born, I have wanted to speak to someone who had first-hand experience of the place. I wanted to know what it may have been like for my mother to have lived there during her confinement and my birth. Naturally, it has taken a little time for anyone to come forward. Today though, I have spoken to a lovely lady who was a resident there, to have her baby in 1966. She does not have good memories of her experience and I suspect that in 1955, just eleven years before, that my mother's experience was not much different and possibly even worse. Why do I want to know what pain my mother suffered, I am not sure, I suppose it is all a part of coming to know her better? Selfishly, I do not want to feel her pain, and yet, I need to understand and really appreciate what she went through for my sake.

The regime was hard, and the routines frequently did not

make sense, for example being woken at six thirty every morning and one poor girl having to get up at least an hour earlier to bring cups of tea up three and four flights of stairs for everyone, despite being heavily pregnant herself. The Austrian cook provided enough food though mostly extremely over-cooked and a constant smell of cabbage hung in the air.

Wooden sinks had to be scrubbed clean daily, along with the cobbled floors, a hands and knees job, the Marley tiles were to be cleaned with 'brillo' pads and the nursery floors swabbed and cleaned with disinfected every day right up until the birth of their baby. Nappies were sluiced and boiled, then put through the twin tub washing machine and hung in covered sheds where they could still get some fresh air to kill off the germs.

In 1966 you arrived at St Olaves six weeks prior to confinement and stayed for six weeks following the birth. You paid nine guineas per week for the privilege, which would have been the equivalent cost of a holiday at a local boarding house. Whilst not cruelly treated, you were seen as sinners. The home was run by the Exeter Diocesan Church of England, and matron was in residence. The attitude of the nurses was not full of compassion. One nurse said to a young mother that if she had wanted to undertake her exams, she should have thought about that before! Another young girl, who had been scrubbing floors the day before, was known to have high blood pressure, which was seen as her norm by the nurse in charge, she had an aneurysm during labour and both she and her baby son died. She was just fifteen years of age. When her blood pressure was checked the previous day, the nurse just said oh, its high again, always is!

Even in the years of 'free love' in the sixties it was still not seen as acceptable to have a baby as a single girl. The girls were encouraged to have their babies adopted even when the fathers were happy to stand by them. Perhaps most of them were young, and not seen as being competent enough to become a mother or a father. There does seem to have been a huge amount of pressure for the babies to be adopted.

The births took place within St Olaves unless there were complications or expected ones; in which case the mothers would be taken to Royal Devon and Exeter or Heavitree hospital, in those days. What a shame that the young girl with high blood pressure was not sent to hospital for a check-up before her confinement. At St. Olaves there were nurses in attendance at the births and doctors called only if required.

Nappies were to be changed on your lap as babies were not to be put down anywhere other than their own cot. Emotional attachments were not encouraged and therefore nor was breast feeding. The first night following the birth, the baby would be kept in another room, and after that you had sole charge for the six weeks, prior to, for most mothers, handing their child over for adoption, resulting in heartbreak for many. Whilst sleeping in dormitories, friendships did not seem to be encouraged between the girls either, all part of the emotional punishment administered through words and actions. In those days there were no counsellors, or support of any kind for the mothers, after all they were sinners! Many families were unaware that their daughters were even having babies. Some girls told their parents that they had a summer job in the West Country or some similar reason for being away from home for several months. My own mother joined a nursing agency in the West Country so that she would go through her pregnancy alone.

Pain relief was given and there was no physical cruelty dealt to the mothers. It reflected the times; and as an unmarried mother many people felt that you had bought shame on the family and had sinned. Thankfully attitudes have changed over the decades.

There was more than one mother and baby home in Exeter, and I have to suppose that the regime was much the same. Others may well have been much worse. It makes me wonder what my mother had to contend with eleven years prior to the lady I have spoken to today. I do know that my mother did not stay at St Olaves after I was three weeks of age, perhaps she managed to find that job in Grayshott which gave her a way out of there. Was it even worse for her because she was older and a qualified nurse, would there have been snide comments, like, she should have known better? Do any of us 'know better' when passion overtakes our usual resolve. None of these mothers deserved to be belittled, judged, or coerced to give up their babies. Thankfully, things have changed. Children and babies, though less of the latter, are still adopted. Breakdowns in adoption are addressed, where in the past they may have been left, leaving children unhappy and alone. The adoption process is far better for the child and hopefully for the natural and the adoptive parents. The stigma has reduced dramatically. Thank goodness.

I feel very privileged that this lady was able and happy to share her personal experience with me and of course has given permission for me to use her experience within this book, along with her poem which I would like to share with you. The poem sums up her thoughts, her personal experience and emotions whilst she was a resident at St Olaves home for fallen girls. She, Maggie was one of the lucky ones, and managed, with the support of her mother, albeit under duress, to keep her baby girl, who now has children of her own.

Alone I entered that awful place,

Silently crying, no tears on my face,

Long narrow corridors filled with gloom,

Sadness pervading every room.

"Abandon hope all ye who enter here"

Was the message, resounding loud and clear.

The wooden sinks, the cobbled floors,

The smell of cabbage that had boiled for hours.

The haunting cries of the young mothers,

Their babies taken, given to others.
Teenage girls filled with fear,
A moment's folly had cost them dear.
Then there was Anne.... she had died in the night,
I cannot forget her, try as I might.
The sight of her parents, white and shaken,
Full of grief, their daughter taken.
Her aorta had burst while she gave birth,
Was this all her life had been worth?
It was here that my first child's life had begun,
A grim beginning for anyone.
The institution is closed now, has long been so,
But my memories, they will never go.

By Maggie P.

Thank you, Maggie, for sharing your experience and reliving those not so happy memories. I really appreciated you talking to me and helping me to put some of my own ghosts to rest.

Chapter 12
The Coachman of Bodryddan Hall

Soon we are due to go up north to visit my father's family and to visit Edna my only surviving relative on my mother's side of the family. On the way we have planned a few days in Wales, to visit the graveyard at Mochdre where my great grandparents are buried and to re-visit St Mary's church at Rhuddlan, along with the village. I have managed to get both death certificates for my great, great, grandparents now and I have sent off for what I hope are their birth certificates. Somehow, I intend to get to the bottom of this family secret, the scandal that Edna is so sure about. So far, all that I can find is that there was at least a twenty-year age gap between my great, great, grand-father and my great, great, grandmother. In the late 1800s I doubt that was particularly strange in the upper classes, though perhaps for working class this may have been more unusual. I am unable to find any marriage certificate, which could suggest that they never actually married though they went on to have seven children together. It could also be that records did sometimes get lost as they were handwritten into books and so could have perished, rather like the records of all the staff at the Hall, during the fire. We are talking about one hundred and sixty-six years ago! I have found recorded births for all their children now and managed to find what seems to be the baptism record for my great, great grandfather Thomas dated fourteenth October 1822, still no birth certificates for either of them which is disappointing. It appears that Thomas' father, Joseph was a Smith, perhaps that is where his love for horses came from.

By using the census documents from 1851 until 1891, I have found that Thomas my great, great, grandfather was groom to Lieutenant John G Crosbie Esq a visitor on the day of the census taken at Bodrhyddan Hall in 1851 when Thomas was single and lodged at the hall. In the 1861 census he was apparently married to Margaret Jane, he was written down as a stableman, living at 'Tele House' and they had two children, Tera aged seven and Thomas aged five. 1871 census shows Thomas and Margaret Jane living at 'Tai Pipes' with five children, Tera does not appear again. Thomas is still noted as a groom, Margaret as a housekeeper, Thomas junior aged fifteen, a servant. I am assuming that at that time both of these properties were on the estate, though now they are apparently no longer part of it. Charlotte appears for the first time aged eight and a scholar, Elizabeth aged five, also a scholar and then Margaret Jane aged three years and Sarah Matilda (my great grandmother) aged nine months. By the time we come to the 1881 census, Charlotte is noted as being a servant at The Hermitage, in Cheshire. Elizabeth Ann now sixteen, is a domestic servant (unemployed), Margaret Jane, fourteen, a scholar, along with Sarah Matilda eleven and Joseph aged seven. Thomas and Margaret Jane are still at the Hall, Thomas listed as groom, and now living at Tilery Cottage in the grounds of the Hall. The 1891 census shows Thomas still as coachman, groom and domestic servant living with Margaret Jane and their youngest son Joseph aged 18 who is working as an agricultural supplement makers Fetler-apprentice. At this stage they have moved to live in the village of Rhuddlan in High Street. Both Margaret Jane and Thomas died in 1893 and they had probably moved to the village to prepare for their retirement. Over the years there were likely to have been land and buildings sold off to protect the ownership of the estate. I assume that the first two properties were on the estate, I do know that Tilery Cottage is still part of the estate and as such may have been required for a younger staff member, though my great, great grandfather still worked at the hall at least two years prior to his death. Did the cottages in Rhuddlan also belong to the estate, perhaps?

Thomas and Margaret Jane must have seen many changes at Bodrhyddan Hall over their thirty plus years of living and working there. The house has a wonderful history and has been in Lord Langford's family for over seven hundred years.

Many changes were made to the architecture of the house in Thomas and Margaret Jane's time, along with the carriage driveway being relocated. It must have been extremely hard work, and exciting at the same time. The 1881 census shows twenty-six staff including five grooms and the coachman. A busy house with guests always shown on the census records.

Along with the information above I think I have found the information about Thomas junior's marriage. I also have marriage and death information for Sarah Matilda, my great grandmother. Without Edna's help I could not have put this story together. Thankfully, Edna had the family information about Thomas and Margaret Jane from her grandparents Sarah Matilda and George, my great grandparents. Margaret Jane had several sisters and Edna remembers seeing photographs of her with her sisters, all dressed beautifully and outside a large house. Edna told me that Thomas and Margaret Jane had eloped and that she, along with her sisters had been the daughter of landed gentry; this memory came from her grandparents Sarah Matilda and George, my great grandparents. This is something we are still trying to get to the core of, to uncover their secret. I have contacted Gretna Green, though sadly their records are only available since 1891, their previous records are few and far between and it is possible that they eloped to Gretna Green for their wedding.

Married or not, and we assume that they were married as they had apparently eloped, they lived happily together and brought up seven children whilst they worked over those thirty years at Bodrhyddan Hall.

Closing the circle

I am so grateful to all the people who have helped and supported me through this journey. I have known my father's family for over twenty years. Finally, after thirty years of searching I have found my mother's family and have the memories and knowledge that Edna has shared with me. I needed to know, about who I am.

Nature and nurture are an interesting subject and I have thought a lot about it whilst writing this book and specifically whilst doing the family research. I was bought up by mum and dad, my adoptive parents who gave me so many opportunities. We enjoyed an extremely healthy outdoor life, of walks, play, garden, and farming. We learnt to ride at a noticeably young age, about four years old, I think. We spent our childhood around animals of all types and used to go out with dad on his veterinary visits. We travelled the world and had a good education. I then went away to work with horses for just over a year at Talland School of Equitation and became a groom as well as achieving my BHSAI (British Horse Society Assistant Instructor) prior to going to college at Norland, to do my NNEB (Nursery nursing). I loved the hospital part of my training as well as all the general childcare and have used that knowledge in my career with children and young people, throughout the services, both statutory and voluntary. I have also been able to combine my opportunities with teaching children to ride. To travel and enjoy the world. And to write about my experiences.

So, how many of the things that I love, are nurture, and now I realise how much is also nature. I am sure there is an equal quantity of both. This journey has been a wonderful and exciting roller coaster, of course there have been frustrations, emotions and tears on the way. I wonder if the insight into the world of my great, great grandmother Margaret Jane's, background and consequent elopement with my great, great grandfather Thomas has perhaps influenced my love of costume drama and latterly 'Downtown Abbey' even more than was already there? Did Thomas influence my lifelong love of horses, did my father Tom, influence my love of travel, or my mother my interest in nursing and childcare. I will never know the answer to those questions, though I can indulge in the belief that all of their influences through nature and the nurture from mum and dad has made me who I am today.

Unfortunately, our visit up to Wales this year has been delayed due to Covid 19, and the lockdown in England along with the fact that both Ian and I are 'shielding', staying away from everyone as much as possible, due to underlying health conditions. We are in our third lockdown now, though as soon as I am able, I will be travelling to Wales to visit Bodrhyddan Hall, Edna in Cheshire and cousin Aggie in Merseyside. That is, after I have been able to hug my children and my grandchildren.

I will walk in my great, great, grandfather and mother's footsteps, I will see where they lived and worked, and that will bring my story to its conclusion, whilst continuing to make memories. I am happy with what I have found out and love the fact that I have a clear picture of my family, on both my father's and my mother's side. I know where I come from and I know that many of their values along with work ethic were on a parallel with my mum and dad who brought me up. A good match indeed.

If you have some mysteries in your family, be brave, follow the leads and learn about where you come from. It is an emotional journey, and yet, well worth taking. DNA testing is a great way to start. I have found a distant American cousin, who has already been to visit; and I will be visiting her in America next year. In the last few weeks, I have been contacted by two additional grandchildren of Tom's, Philip and Louise, who originate from St Helen's only a few miles from my father's hometown. To date, Tom had four children, eight grandchildren and eleven great grandchildren. How sad that he did not know any of us as a father, grandfather or great grandfather. I am pleased to say that through the family, I have come to know him. I have a great respect for his contribution during the war, and from his siblings I have only ever heard of their love for him. There are some aspects of his life and particularly his lack of responsibility where the women and the children in his life were concerned, that I am not so proud of. We all have our skeletons and I truly believe that his experiences in the war, must have affected his ability to make life-time commitments. He is my father, and I am pleased to have been able to know him. I do however, wonder sometimes how many more of his offspring might make contact through DNA testing!

My mother was caring, quiet and brave, she had such hard decisions to make, and whilst she had the emotional support of her family, they were unable to help in a physical sense, she knew that she could not give me the life she wanted for me. I am so very sorry, and sad that I did not make the connections in time to meet her. I would love to have told her that I had a good life, with so many opportunities and experiences. I would like to have talked to her about so many issues and to have asked her about her relationship with my father, introduced her to her grandchildren and great grandchildren. Whilst my mother did not speak about my adoption once it had been finalised, I am sure that she would have had thoughts about my life, certainly on my birth date, and whether perhaps she had grandchildren somewhere in the world. So sad that she had no more children herself, and that her marriage to Frank was for such a short time. I am so thankful to Edna for all that she has been able to share with me about my mother, her character, her career, her life and her relationship with Tom. He continued to be in touch with my mother, Margaret, for five years that we know of, he must have cared for her greatly. Did she ever tell him about me, I wonder?

My journey has been a wonderful cultural recipe for me. I had all the basic ingredients from the nurture perspective; and as my journey progressed, I collected a concoction from the nature tray, through meeting more and more family members. All of these disparate elements have combined to make my journey of discovery a truly life-affirming experience. Perhaps you have your own journey waiting for you ....

There are still some questions, some mysteries, and I am ok with that, because that is how it should be. Few of us know everything about our families and perhaps some secrets are best kept hidden.

Thomas, Catherine and Margaret brought together through the Secrets of the Quill Box. Photos taken of Thomas in NZ 1955/57, Margaret in Chester June 1955 and Catherine August 1956.

Who am I?

I am the person whose roots have grown stronger, deeper, and more resilient

I am the person whose branches have strength, resolve, and reach towards the clouds

I am me

I know who I am

Cathy lives and works in Cornwall, where she lectured at a local college, in Child Care and Education for ten years before returning to work in Children's Services. Now retired she is the author of 'Out of the Quill Box, Came Secrets of a Family I had Never Known'.

Cathy has been writing for about five years and written two short books, both non-fictions, 'White Horses and Sunbeams' her first book is about family and being brought up in Cornwall. A story of four generations who have lived in, worked, and enjoyed the diversity that this beautiful county has to offer.

The second, recently published, 'Matt and Pandora' is about one of her grandsons, his passion for horse riding and how he builds a beautiful, trusting relationship with his very first pony, Pandora. She has also written articles for an online foster care magazine.

Cathy also worked with the fostering team and was a council foster carer for several years. She is only too aware of the importance of information for children and young people, to know their past, their heritage, and their culture.

Printed in Great Britain
by Amazon